Attached to the Li

a new
ECOPOETRY
anthology

EDITED BY

Ann Fisher-Wirth and
Laura-Gray Street

Foreword by Camille Dungy
Introduction by Margaret Ronda

TERRA FIRMA BOOKS | TRINITY UNIVERSITY PRESS
San Antonio, Texas

Terra Firma Books, an imprint of
Trinity University Press
San Antonio, Texas 78212

Book design by BookMatters, Berkeley
Cover design by Derek Thornton / Notch Design
Cover art: Giant sequoia towering above surrounding forest and person at its
base. Colored lithograph after W. P. Blake, c. 1857. Rawpixel/13965699.

ISBN 978-1-59534-308-6 paper
ISBN 978-1-59534-310-9 ebook

Trinity University Press strives to produce its books using methods and
materials in an environmentally sensitive manner. We favor working with
manufacturers that practice sustainable management of all natural resources,
produce paper using recycled stock, and manage forests with the best possible
practices for people, biodiversity, and sustainability. The press is a member of
the Green Press Initiative, a nonprofit program dedicated to supporting pub-
lishers in their efforts to reduce their impacts on endangered forests, climate
change, and forest-dependent communities.

The paper used in this publication meets the minimum requirements of the
American National Standard for Information Sciences—Permanence of Paper
for Printed Library Materials, ansi 39.48–1992.

Printed in Canada

CIP data on file at the Library of Congress

29 28 27 26 25 | 5 4 3 2 1

For all beings

CONTENTS

Foreword, by Camille Dungy · *xix*

Introduction, by Margaret Ronda · *xxi*

Santiago Acosta
Never Surrender Your Heart to a Nuclear Power Plant · *1*

Kelli Russell Agodon
In the Next 50 Years So Many Animals Will Go Extinct It Will Take
Earth at Least 3 Million Years to Recover · *3*

Hussain Ahmed
Talking Drums II · *4*
Cosmology of Extinction · *5*

Ashia Ajani
Blue Cascade · *6*
Mint · *7*

Ellery Akers
Rachel Carson · *8*

Ruth Awad
Hunger · *10*
The Years of Water & Light · *11*

Subhaga Crystal Bacon
Warming, Cooling; Wet, Dry: Burning Haibun · *12*

David Baker
Extinction · *13*

Ned Balbo
A Spell for Lamentation and Renewal · *14*
The Wolves of Chernobyl · *15*

Stacey Balkun
The Water, the Truth, the Water · *16*
In the Forest · *17*

Mildred Kinonco Barya
Cast Over Gorée Island · *18*

Janée J. Baugher
Andrew Wyeth's Footnotes to *Frosted Apples*, 1967 · *19*
Andrew Wyeth's Footnotes to *The Carry*, 2003 · *20*

Anna Lena Phillips Bell
Emerald · *21*

Jared Beloff
The Bird Collector · *22*

Ariana Benson
Black Pastoral · *23*
Love Poem in the Black Field · *24*

Sherwin Bitsui
from Dissolve
[A field that shivered with a thousand cranes] · *25*
[On limbs of slanted light] · *25*

Allen Braden
Inspiration · *26*

Tina Mozelle Braziel
  What the Creek Says · *27*

Nickole Brown
  A Prayer to Talk to Animals · *28*
  Collective Nouns for the Anthropocene · *29*

B. J. Buckley
  Pronghorn Elegy · *31*

Simmons Buntin
  Desert Cottontail · *32*

Lauren Camp
  I've started naming the landscape: sweet · *33*
  Echinopsis Pachanoi · *34*

Wendy Taylor Carlisle
  May We in This Time · *35*

Anders Carlson-Wee
  Trash · *36*

Emogene Cataldo
  A question about procreation as the rivers dry · *37*

Victoria Chang
  The Ocean · *38*
  Touching the Tree · *39*

Robin Chapman
  That slant of sun · *40*

Teresa Mei Chuc
  Mother of Waters, River of Nine Dragons · *41*
  Chernobyl Necklace · *42*

Anthony Cody
  brd · *43*

Daniel Corrie
Wiregrass, Bluestem, Indian Grass, Palmetto, Ferns, Wildflowers,
Blackberry, Gallberry, Longleaf Pine, the Sweep of Fire · 45

Britney Corrigan
The Strip Mall Changes Its Mind · 46
Anthropocene Blessing: California Condor · 47

jason b. crawford
A Double Sonnet for the River · 48

Laura Da'
An Unknowable Creator Departs the Talking Fields · 49
The Meadow Views: Sword and Symbolic History · 50

Aidan Daniel
Virginia Possum Rages · 52

Noah Davis
Poem Sewn into My Hunting Jacket · 53

Todd Davis
Apostate · 54

Lucille Lang Day
Lost Languages · 55

Janine DeBaise
Woven · 56

Natalie Diaz
The First Water Is the Body · 57

LaTasha N. Nevada Diggs
ᎤᏪᏴ uweyvi is Tsalagi for river · 63

Michael Dowdy
Blast Fragments · 64

Kendall Dunkelberg
The intergalactic traveler in springtime · 65

The intergalactic traveler tells it like it is · *66*

Iris Jamahl Dunkle
Black Blizzard · *67*
Disaster, a Reckoning · *68*

Thomas Dunn
It was raining · *69*

Teresa Dzieglewicz
Baking Bread as Oceti Sakowin Is Raided · *70*

Martín Espada
Love Song of the Galápagos Tortoise · *74*

Michelle Bonczek Evory
By root, by petal, by sword · *75*

Alyson Favilla
Bullfrog · *76*

Beth Ann Fennelly
The Last Hummingbird of Summer · *77*

Molly Fisk
August · *78*

Vievee Francis
Clarity (for Those Who Do Nothing but Hope) · *79*
Cruelty · *79*

CMarie Fuhrman
End Times · *80*
Questioning the Sun · *81*

Benjamin Garcia
Reasons for Abolishing Ice · *82*

Michael Garrigan
Liturgy of Carp Becoming a God · *83*

Ross Gay
A Small Needful Fact · *84*
Becoming a Horse · *85*

Melissa Ginsburg
So attached you are to living in the world · *86*

Sarah Giragosian
Newtok, Alaska · *87*

Jody Gladding
[grass widow / grass stained] · *88*

Rigoberto González
from Apocalipsixtlán
[5. Signs of the End of the World] · *89*
[12. A Second Crack in the Earth] · *90*

Andrew Gottlieb
The Inner Wild · *92*

Robin Gow
Kill Your Local Lanternfly · *93*
Lanternflies Dream of Being Butterflies · *94*

Maggie Graber
in which i notice the birds again · *95*

Dana J. Graef
On the Creek · *96*

Miriam Bird Greenberg
• [Whole towns like • horses turnt loose] · *97*
• [In Paradise the fire ate] · *98*

Lilace Mellin Guignard
Fracked Pastoral · *99*

Kelsea Habecker
Self-Portrait with Salmon · *101*

Aaron Hand
Glimpses of Wilderness · *102*

Eman Hassan
To the Beach with My Nephew · *103*

Gisela Heffes
An Epistemology of Floriculture · *104*

Kathleen Hellen
big weary · *106*

W. J. Herbert
The End of Immortality · *108*

Claudia D. Hernández
The River Never Happened to Us (ii.) · *109*

Tiffany Margaret Higgins
Chewing the Sun · *110*

Sean Hill
The White-Headed Woodpecker · *112*

Rick Hilles
Tell Me · *113*

Caroline Hockenbury
Machete · *115*

Cynthia Marie Hoffman
Ecotherapy · *117*

Marybeth Holleman
she *zompopas* · *119*

Erin Coughlin Hollowell
Wrack Line · *121*
Choreographic · *122*

Marie Howe
Postscript · *123*

Richard Jackson
An Ending of Sorts · 124

Jessica Jacobs
And the Ground Opens Its Mouth to Speak · 126

Elizabeth Jacobson
There Are as Many Songs in the World as Branches of Coral · 128

Jacqueline Johnson
Wild Life · 132

Taylor Johnson
Consider the Deer · 133
from Hymn · 133

Ever Jones
Overheard from the Field · 136

Kasey Jueds
The Vultures · 138

Joan Naviyuk Kane
To List · 140
Darker Passage · 141

Julia Spicher Kasdorf
A Mother Near the West Virginia Line Considers the Public
Health · 143

Athena Kildegaard
Sudden · 146

Grant Kittrell
the plan was to build the pipeline through my left lung · 147

Sophie Klahr
Tender · 148

Christopher Kondrich
Endling · 149

Brandon Krieg
　Invasives · *150*

Petra Kuppers
　Found on the Pond Deck · *152*
　Found on Mushrooming Walk · *152*

Joe M. Lamb
　Trinity · *153*

John Lane
　Elegy for Sugar Sand and Slash Pine · *154*

J. Drew Lanham
　from Bird Watching: Four Poems for Dead Negroes
　　[2. What the Starling Said] · *156*
　　[3. Why the Whip-poor-will Wept] · *157*

Deborah Leipziger
　Lobo · *159*

Julia Levine
　Milk · *161*

Rossy Lima
　Water Path / *Aguacamino* · *163*

Ada Limón
　Drowning Creek · *165*
　The Carrying · *166*

Layli Long Soldier
　Steady Summer · *167*
　from Whereas · *170*

Sandy Longhorn
　The Crumple Zone · *171*

Éireann Lorsung
　Garden cycle (keeping time) · *173*

Lea Marshall
    Future Folk Tales: Fox · *175*
    Future Folk Tales: Fireflies · *176*

Jennifer Martelli
    Snakes · *177*

Airea D. Matthews
    His Eye on the Sparrow · *178*

Janet McAdams
    Earthling · *179*

Anne Haven McDonnell
    Once There Were Fish · *180*
    Inside a lateness, a singing under snow · *181*

Rose McLarney
    Fresh Tracks · *183*

Lucien Darjeun Meadows
    Violet · *184*
    Mile 57— · *185*

Rajiv Mohabir
    Why Whales Are Back in New York City · *186*
    Stomach Full of Trash · *187*

Daniela Naomi Molnar
    Memory of a larger mind · *188*

Sawnie Morris
    Frog Song · *189*

Aimee Nezhukumatathil
    Mr. Cass and the Crustaceans · *191*
    Triggerfish Invective · *192*

January Gill O'Neil
    The River Remembers · *193*

Cecily Parks
    Girlhood · *194*

Lynn Pattison
    When even the north grew too hot · *195*

Andrew Payton
    War Road · *196*

Tommy Pico
    from Nature Poem · *197*

Catherine Pierce
    Anthropocene Pastoral · *201*

Arlene Plevin
    Tikkun Olam · *202*

Vivian Faith Prescott
    How to Yoik the Stikine River · *204*
    At a nearby glacier, I heard a yoik for a child · *205*

Jessica Purdy
    After Watching Lior Patel's "Aerial Timelapse of Sheep Herding" and
        Søren Solkær's "Amorphous Flocks of Starlings Swell above the
        Danish Marshlands" · *206*

Jane Satterfield
    Emily Brontë's Advice for the Anthropocene · *208*

Rebecca Seiferle
    In the unending rain · *209*

Alafia Nicole Sessions
    Love Poem as Omnipastoral · *212*

Leona Sevick
    Fallout · *214*

Samyak Shertok
    The Last Beekeeper · *215*
    A Brief History of Hunger · *216*

John Shoptaw
  Pangolin Scales · *217*

Martha Silano
  Self-Portrait as Southern Resident Orca · *219*

Dorsía Smith Silva
  Hurricane María Countdown · *221*
  I pause to give gratitude to green · *222*

Jake Skeets
  In the Fields · *223*
  Anthropocene: A Dictionary · *224*

Danez Smith
  dear white america · *225*
  dream where every black person is standing by the ocean · *226*

Tracy K. Smith
  An Old Story · *227*

Heidi Staples
  Prayer · *228*

Page Starzinger
  Galaxy Filament · *229*

Rose Strode
  Saint Cuthbert Proclaims the First Sanctuary for Birds, 676 A.D. · *230*

Marcela Sulak
  Lantana · *231*

Heather Swan
  After · *232*

Tess Taylor
  from California Suites
    [I. Rainy Season] · *233*
    [IV. Escrow] · *233*

Brian Teare

from Toxics Release Inventory · 235

Orchid Tierney

from a field guide to future flora
[cottonwood or microfleece] · 240
[flowers are slow-moving cows of the glebe] · 241

Alison Townsend

Northern Red Oak: Mercy · 242

Natasha Trethewey

Elegy [I think by now the river must be thick] · 243

Brian Turner

The Immortals · 245
One Last Moment in the Vast City of Ants · 246

Susan Underwood

God as the Nest of Rabbits We Girls Found While Camping at My
Cousin Carmen's · 248

Mai Der Vang

After All Have Gone · 249

Irene Vázquez

Hothouse or, The Taking Back of the Provision Grounds · 250

Joe Wilkins

Explain: Wolves · 253

Corrie Williamson

Mercy Me · 254

Cathy Wittmeyer

Genesis 2:20 · 256

Karenne Wood

from The Naming · 257

Diana Woodcock
    Hippocampus (Bent Horse) · 258

William Woolfitt
    The Night the Rain Had Nowhere to Go · 260

Ellen June Wright
    Who's to say my body is not all the world · 261

Kenton K. Yee
    The Big One · 262

Monica Youn
    A Guide to Usage: Mine · 264

Felicia Zamora
    Ecogodliness · 266

Jessica Zhou
    Southeastern Expansion · 267

Karl Zuelke
    Cat o' the Mountain · 269

Jane Zwart
    I read that the moon is rusting · 270

Contributors' Notes · 271
Acknowledgments and Credits · 285

FOREWORD

Camille Dungy

I am excited about the expansive intelligence and compassionate aware-
ness in *Attached to the Living World*, which is a kind of companion to *The
Ecopoetry Anthology*, published in 2013. Excited but not surprised. Many of
these poets are not new to my attentions and affections, and though some
of these poems may feel as if they only recently floated into the world, the
concerns presented here have weighed heavy on my mind for what feels
like a very long time.

I recall being part of a conversation early in my acquaintance with
Laura-Gray Street, one of the editors of *The Ecopoetry Anthology*. Street's
enthusiasm bubbled as brightly as the brook near her backyard as she told
our group about an exciting new community of writers: bloggers. This was
before such web-based communication was a norm, so Street offered us a
welcoming definition. "Like a captain's log, a journal, but on the Web," she
explained. "Weblog." Perhaps this anecdote makes Street and the group she
spoke with sound ancient, but that assessment would depend somewhat
on your perspective of time. As Victoria Chang reminds us in one of the
poems in this magnificent new anthology, "The oldest tree is / five thou-
sand years old." By that measure, the word *blog*, which first came into use
around 1999, is very new, but as a ship log is linked to a Substack post, or
a magnolia sapling is linked to the first flowering trees, new words—and
new poems—are rooted in a long tradition. If my focus on the early days
of the technologically driven world feels out of place in the foreword to a
collection of ecopoetry, note the reminder from Natalie Diaz that technol-
ogy is the cause of, and for some the possible solution to, many of the

environmental catastrophes faced on the planet today. The poems collected here register what is happening in the world and what direction we should take as we move forward. Like any useful log, *Attached to the Living World* reveals crucial connections through time, space, knowledge, grief, and care.

Laura-Gray Street and Ann Fisher-Wirth began thinking seriously about collecting poems for *The Ecopoetry Anthology* in the early 2000s. In that time, while people might have been able to define *environmental writing* or *nature poetry*, the word *ecopoetry* was as unfamiliar to many as the word *blog*. The world was changing rapidly—perhaps catastrophically. We needed new language and renewed imagination to register what we saw and felt and knew. In those early years, Street and Fisher-Wirth offered useful definitions and examples of the rapidly developing poetic mode *ecopoetry*. But Street and Fisher-Wirth have not remained satisfied with a limited and limiting representation of the community of writers working in the mode. *Attached to the Living World* opens this necessary conversation to an even wider audience, welcoming poets who were too young to have had work included in the 2013 book, poets who might not have identified as ecopoets in those early years, and poets whose work, for a variety of reasons, had not yet come to the editors' attention. I am delighted by the welcoming breadth of this anthology's scope.

So much of the world shows up in the renewed record registered on these pages. Many countries, many peoples, many greater-than-human life forces are here. These poems exhibit a wide-ranging curiosity, shifting their forms, their tones, and their focus in countless ways so that what seems old might be renewed, what seems disconnected might connect, and what seems lost might be remembered. I celebrate *Attached to the Living World*. Highest praise to the expanding definitions for communication, concern, and care this book welcomes into the world.

INTRODUCTION

Margaret Ronda

In her poem "A Prayer to Talk to Animals," Nickole Brown writes: "There is a sorrow on the air / I taste but cannot name." Brown's poem, included in *Attached to the Living World*, offers a powerful meditation on the capacities and limits of language in a time of climate alteration and species extinction. How can we sense, or "taste," a perception of grief that defies total understanding? What does "the air" bear as a holder of unpredictable, even catastrophic change? And how might poetry be a means of attunement to these difficult and refractory realities, to the conditions and experiences of climate grief?

Brown's poem captures a longing *in* language *for* language that could adequately address this predicament, and that could speak beyond the divisions and forms of violence that separate humans from other earthly beings. The poem closes with these lines:

> I want to open
> my mouth and know the exact
> flavor of what's to come, I want to open
> my mouth and sound a language
> that calls all language home.

In Brown's poem, poetry becomes a key space for meditating on forms of language that might unite and draw together, expressing a wish for what might be. At the same time, the poem provides an acknowledgment of real alienation from other species, a reckoning with loss, and explores feelings of anticipation and dread for "what's to come." The poem's language of desire, voicing, and sorrow frames it as a contemporary, secular prayer, a call to something beyond rational comprehension for sustenance and strength amid a time of great existential challenge.

Brown's poetic inquiry into what language can and cannot hold, into what can and cannot be named, offers one illuminating window into the urgent, moving explorations of poetry and environment gathered in *Attached to the Living World*, a companion to *The Ecopoetry Anthology*, editors Ann Fisher-Wirth and Laura-Gray Street's groundbreaking first volume. Published in 2013, *The Ecopoetry Anthology* continues to be an essential resource of environmental anglophone poetry from modernist works to selected contemporary poems.

This second anthology focuses squarely on the poetry of our current moment. Fisher-Wirth and Street have collected a diverse array of poems by well-known and emerging poets that demonstrate the remarkable range of approaches contemporary ecopoetry in English presents. From engagements with traditional forms such as dramatic monologue, pastoral, elegy, sonnet, and ode to more experimental modes like documentary, experimental sound play, and concrete poems, today's ecopoetry engages with myriad elements of poetic form and pattern, and expands them to evoke new ideas, realities, and responses.

Global Crisis, Terrains of Response

The poems in *Attached to the Living World* broadly reflect imaginative meditations on the planetary crisis we face, generated by the ongoing dynamics of colonial and capitalist development and the accelerating use of fossil fuels. This crisis takes a variety of forms, and its effects are evident in every planetary cycle and sphere. From species extinction and habitat loss to changes in the nitrogen cycle, from warming oceans and coral die-off to polluted rivers and cancer clusters, megastorms, droughts, and wildfires to shrinking glaciers, the effects of anthropogenic changes to the earth system are pervasive. And these varied and interlocking forms of environmental transformation continue to intensify. The year 2023 was named the hottest year on the planetary record, and conditions such as ocean acidification, deforestation, plastic pollution, soil depletion, and food insecurity are worsening.

The poems collected here are deeply attuned to these overlapping and intensifying forms of crisis. The anthology lays out a broad terrain of poetic thinking, formal and thematic, on these elements of crisis. They meditate on different scales and tempos of earth system transformation, charting accelerating speeds of biospheric change or chronicling the remaindered forms of toxic industrial cycles. In "Ocean," Victoria Chang pens an imagined obituary for the sea. In "Toxics Release Inventory," Brian Teare writes of contaminants inhabiting bodies and circulating in air: "when industry goes / so wide, so deep, & touches / us so totally." A variety of poems meditate on species extinction and endangerment or explore forms of alienation from animal life. Hussein Ahmed's "Cosmology of Extinction" offers a powerful parable of various species dying out, past and present. Lucille Lang Day's "Lost Languages" connects the extinction of languages and species as a catastrophic waning of planetary biodiversity. Other poems, such as Subhaga Crystal Bacon's "Warming, Cooling; Wet, Dry: Burning Haibun" or Rebecca Seiferle's "In the unending rain," depict unsettling or turbulent weather patterns that register wider climatic disruption.

These epochal changes have been categorized as part of the Anthropocene, a term coined by atmospheric chemist Paul Crutzen and botanist Eugene Stoermer to define a geological era measured by the predominant effects of humans as a species on the global environment. Climate scientists and geologists continue to debate the Anthropocene's time frame. The concept has found its way into urgent conversations in the humanities and social sciences, becoming an influential, if controversial, framework for understanding the planetary scale of anthropogenic environmental alteration.

In *Attached to the Living World*, poets draw explicitly on this term to indicate the ways this concept reshapes our awareness of collective presents and horizons. In "Anthropocene Pastoral," Catherine Pierce describes the eerie beauty of warming seasons and disrupted phenological cycles through the lens of pastoral: "One New Year's Day we woke / to daffodils, wisteria, oniongrass wafting / through the open windows." The poem ends with a collective apology to the surroundings, offering an ironized refiguring of pastoral in a time of climate change: "*I'm sorry, I'm so sorry*, while petals / sifted softly to the ground all around us." In "Anthropocene: A Dictionary," Jake Skeets draws on Navajo words to depict a scene of wildfire conflagration that evokes broader catastrophe: ": *deidíítid*, they burned it / : *kódeiilyaa*, we did this." Both poems offer insight into the imaginative scales and questions of culpability that the Anthropocene's epochal transformations demand. They register the ways poetic language gives distinctive voice to these horizons of thought.

Environmental Injustice and Poetic Witness

Environmental humanities and postcolonial scholars have pointed out the ways a universalizing Anthropocene discourse can elide key forms of inequality, environmental racism, and the uneven distribution of climate risk. Reflecting this fact, numerous poems in *Attached to the Living World* convey powerful reckonings with forms of environmental racism and climate injustice, whether by turning to personal narrative or poetry of witness or by employing more exploratory techniques, pointing out how ecological crises reflect systems of domination and exploitation that affect marginalized populations disproportionately. Some poems address issues of climate migration and displacement, the effects of fracking on rural and impoverished communities, or experiences of solastalgia for landscapes transformed by extractive economies. Others chronicle protest movements such as Standing Rock, as in Teresa Dzieglewicz's "Baking Bread as Oceti Sakowin Is Raided."

These poems share a sense that poetry can develop modes of witness to make visible the relations between environmental and social injustice, and that poetry's vivid, intense, memorable language produces forms of testimony and response to such injustice. Ruth Awad's "Hunger" forcefully reckons with economic and environmental injustice, reflecting on the realities of food insecurity and poverty in terms at once personal and global. Meditating on a memory of her father stealing an apple, Awad writes, "If you steal an apple, it's a crime. / If you withhold an apple from someone who's hungry, it's not." Another poem, Benjamin Garcia's "Reasons for Abolishing Ice," uses "ice" as a refrain to examine the interconnected experiences of systemic racism, carceral and border violence, and climate injustice. Playing on the multiple meanings and presences of ice—as an increasingly depleted dimension of glaciers and as the acronym for the U.S. Immigration and Customs Enforcement department, Garcia plays on paradox and irony: "because they say the polar caps aren't melting   ice / because a person could slip through at any moment   ice."

Various poems in *Attached to the Living World* speak to structural forms of anti-Black racism and violence as indelibly linked to environmental concerns. Ross Gay's "A Small Needful Fact" reframes the violent killing of Eric Garner by New York City police officers, drawing attention instead to Garner's employment in the horticulture department for New York's parks. With care and precision, Gay underscores the way Garner's gardening work continues to reverberate, creating livable habitats and air to breathe for the citizens of the city. Ariana Benson's haunting poem "Black Pastoral" juxtaposes histories of lynching and ongoing racist violence alongside tender images of the young lives of a Black boy and a young deer, asking: "Who among you would interrupt this pastoral? Who would muddy // these budding strokes with pigment too dense for the canvas?" These poems, and many others in the anthology, express a language of loving care for both Black life and the natural world amid ongoing conditions of systemic racial violence and environmental depletion.

Poems of Connection and Praise

If an overarching theme of the ecopoetry gathered here is the question of how to reckon with ecological loss, destruction, and various forms of violence, an equally central component is the need to imagine forms of renewal, to foster hope, and to rekindle a sense of wonder in relation to the nonhuman environment. Some poems highlight the connection between body and ecology to celebrate the shared vitality of ecological existence. Ellen June Wright's "who's to say my body is not the world" offers a praise poem in these terms, celebrating Black women's power and strength as coextensive with the wildness and complexity of the natural world. She writes:

who's to say my big, brown
        body is not the whole world
            with its hemispheres, equator
                its longitude and latitude
            its mighty meridian

Other works describe practices of noticing and learning about the natural world—its cycles, its intricate webs of relation. Some involve becoming newly attentive to the animal world and to forms of creaturely behavior and interaction. Others portray acts of listening or looking with renewed attention or seeing anew a familiar place or everyday encounter. As Maggie Graber writes in "in which i notice the birds again," "here is the fire, the forest / & the garden. here are the birds again. i know / some of their names." Poems like these cultivate the difficult, necessary art of embodied daily attention to the relations and entities that create and sustain life. Still others draw readers to moments of hope or inspiration, such as Aimee Nezhukumatathil's "Mr. Cass and the Crustaceans," about her fourth-grade science teacher who inspired her to keep learning about biology. "How I wish I could tell Mr. Cass / how I've never stopped checking the waters— / the ponds, the lakes, the sea," she writes.

Several poems convey the relational ecological practices embedded in the lifeways and ontologies of Indigenous communities. In "The First Water Is the Body," Natalie Diaz offers a particularly evocative exploration of the intimate interconnection between river, body, community, and language for the Mojave people: "I carry a river. It is who I am: 'Aha Makav. This is not metaphor. / When a Mojave says, *Inyech 'Aha Makavch ithuum*, we are saying our name. / We are telling a story of our existence. *The river runs through the middle of my body*." She refuses the mediations of metaphor, insisting instead on the identity of river and people and highlighting how language can be a vehicle for exploring such forms of coextensiveness. Poetry, in turn, becomes a space for bearing this language of interrelation, for naming presence and also for grieving loss and resisting colonial domination. Diaz continues: "If I say, *My river is disappearing*, do I also mean, *My people are disappearing*?" In "Exceeding Beringia," Inupiaq poet Joan Naviyuk Kane evokes the layered worlds of ancestral and present land: "This land with its laws that serve as wire / and root to draw us together." Here, land at once evokes displacement and a site of return and new homemaking, inextricably connected to community lifeways. The poems by Native poets in this anthology underscore the holistic awareness of environmental coexistence central to Indigenous storytelling and poetic forms past and present. They testify to the ongoing legacies of colonial violence that have ruptured and transformed these relations. And they highlight resilience, restoration, and return as key elements of ecological and cultural continuance. Kane writes at the end of "Exceeding Beringia" of a shared communal return "to wear another furrow, to make portage, / to make our land our home anew."

Future Visions

While some poems describe environmental conditions of the present in their complexity and contradiction, some explore visions of what the future might hold. Poems like Rigoberto González's "Apocalipsixtlán" conjure apocalyptic or diminished horizons. Others provide vantages into more hopeful or equivocal prospects. A poem like Orchid Tierney's "a field guide to future flora" reimagines the field guide in an uncanny and wild remix of entangled life. Tracy K. Smith's "An Old Story" presents a parable of transformation that intimates the possibility of reprieve and restoration in the wake of terrible calamity. Britney Corrigan's "The Strip Mall Changes Its Mind" envisions the suburban mall as a space of future rewilding, where foxes move in and the stars become visible through the collapsed roof. Ecological replenishment in the wake of human development and disappearance offers a glimpse of what a posthuman landscape might look like. Such poems foster diverse speculative vocabularies and imaginative repertoires, conceiving potential futures that range from bleak to heartening.

The ecopoems in *Attached to the Living World*, whether oriented toward the future or offering narratives and images of our present, at once explore and enact the work that poetic language can do—to quicken attention, to give voice to affective responses, to forge and sustain relationships, to witness, to protest and demand justice, to reimagine and renew. They register the affective responses that emerge in response to these conditions, from grief to bewilderment to rage. They generate feelings of hope, wonder, and awe as necessary responses to the beauty and complexity of the nonhuman world that sustains us. And they attend to entanglement and interconnection, to alienation and loss, to create striking, beautiful forms and patterns that impart shape and meaning to the ecological experience. Amid a time of immense challenge, they provide passionate and vital visions to nurture our imaginations and spur us to act.

Santiago Acosta

Never Surrender Your Heart to a Nuclear Power Plant

The bars are already closing.

From the window of the taxi taking me home, I see the city lights
gleaming on the bay.

On my right, luxury apartments, completely empty.

No one dreams of living by the sea anymore.

The storm took out almost all the subway lines.

Long rows of tractors struggle in vain to dig out collapsed tunnels, but
the salt doesn't stop its own digging into the steel beams and rails.

Still, people keep on drinking and mingling and falling helplessly in love.

And to smoke unconcerned on balconies while, under the ashes, the
urban grid collapses.

Many assure that there is nothing to fear, that events are overblown by
the news and general anxiety.

It is four in the morning and I am moving through a river of the faithful,
who carry banners of the Virgin Mary, hop on and off trucks and
buses, then walk across the highway at two degrees below zero.

Who am I to question the norms of despair?

The taxi driver pushes on in suspicious silence, as if keeping a state
secret.

As if he understood the purpose of the recent floods.

There's always someone coming up to us, asking us to stay a little longer,
don't leave, the party's just getting started.

But I can't stop thinking of the arrogance of owning a house with an
ocean view.

In the Middle Ages, inhabitants along the Fukushima coast placed stone
tablets with clear warnings everywhere:

Do not build on this coast | Tsunami risk.

Today, radioactive currents have hit the beaches of California, Mexico, and Peru.

The Great Pacific Garbage Patch is already beginning to dissolve from the effect of the isotopes.

Hundreds of families line up at government offices, affected by the same radiation that makes the guts of fish glow.

The television in the waiting room shows images of a newly open refinery built near the border.

The gas flares have been digitally erased, and now the refinery stands innocuously against a perfect blue sky.

No one notices the ambassador passing by, dragging a sack of yams covered with tar.

The taxi driver hits the gas, making the long night of crisis even darker.

I turn up the volume on my headphones to torment myself with the synthesizers and bass lines.

I don't want to hear the groaning of my drunken belly.

No one dreams of waking up in front of the sea anymore.

I don't mind carrying the parasite of melancholy in my gut.

The beaches will burn to bid us farewell.

— Translated by Tiffany Troy

Kelli Russell Agodon

In the Next 50 Years So Many Animals Will Go Extinct It Will Take Earth at Least 3 Million Years to Recover

I'm not writing about the wisteria
because I'm concerned about the heart
murmur in the thimbleberries.
My least favorite flower is a freeway,
my least favorite freeway is a wall.
Once I took a nap in a field of bees
and all my dreams were sweet and buzzing.
How can we pollinate the earth
if we're all asleep? Let me tuck myself
into the bee balm, let me, like a tree frog, fall
asleep on a leaf. The sky is a novel rewriting
itself with clouds. I'm not writing about the
sky because there's an inchworm on my
coffee spoon. What are we measuring out
today? The size
of a waxwing's heart is the same size
as a sigh. But what else
can the birds do, the wisteria is also dying,
and still they sing and sing and sing.

Hussain Ahmed

Talking Drums II

When a river disappears,
It springs up
On another planet.
After hundreds of years
A new moon will be
Discovered with its many
Lakes and oceans
Or beach with footprints
That resembles mine.
A fish skin is waterproof,
And could be made into a drum
That will sing of the river
When it was an hourglass
Shrinking but being cheered
For the unconventional shape
Before a lake dries up,
It mimics a drum, say gangan.
In another life, a sword's grip
Is made of a cod skin,
As a tribute to the river
And the borders it carved.

Cosmology of Extinction

Every ocean that has tried to kill me was made stronger,
except when a ship breaks down in the middle of it,

leaking black oil into the coral reef. How do I rescue
what is rendered homeless without crossing the border?

The oil film concealed the sunlight from the photic zone,
until savaged, a blood moon sits over the ocean.

On this day, two centuries away, I imagined
a boy my age rescued a Quagga from drowning,

feathers of a dodo clenched between his teeth,
this was before petals of viola-cryana withered inside a lighthouse.

On the same day, the snores of whales were halved
by flapping rotor blades, and the sputtering water sounds like a lullaby

to the ears of a dying orangutan. Dandelions were planted
on the graves of elephants buried without their tusks.

Shadows clustered inside an amphitheatre, with every death
a flute is emptied of its music, in a foundry for ghosts.

Ashia Ajani

Blue Cascade

Are you sure, sweetheart, that you want to be well?
— TONI CADE BAMBARA

When a chimpanzee is feeling ill,
it will chew on willow leaves to draw out the salicylic acid.
Dolphins rub themselves against puffer fish to get high—white people
take ayahuasca in the Amazon to purge their colonial guilt &
my cat chews on my roommate's monstera to induce vomiting.
What I mean to say is, we are all looking for ways to self-soothe:
expunge or embed. I am convinced octopi punch fish
not out of spite, but release, the same way my greedy fingers
seem to find their way to the space between cotton & clit
every evening. Like the orcas' impulse, my desire sits
at the border between play & vengeance.

In late spring, a man with locs he retwists himself
plants sunflowers to draw up lead from the soil. In a neighborhood
plagued by history, patience matters more than power. He shoos
away the zombies dropping needles in the alley with a
"You ain't gotta go home but you can't stay here" but please
take some vegetables with you, you'll need the iron. There is no quick fix
to hollow, but wholeness may submerge you in graygreen quiet. Cortez
sings the blue-ooze, burdened with memory, dispersed like aerosols—
They come because it is the softest place available. Less
than a month before, someone was talked down from the Bay Bridge
eager to become one with the sea. You know, the myth where
enslaved Africans just got so fed up they surrendered to the sky & just
flew up on out of there, buoyed by ocean spray. Soon,
we will all be a little closer to Atlantis. The coastline erodes into a
Black expanse, the soil turned too salty to yield any medicine.
Tender zone in the seam of asphalt & marshland reveals a city's
green yearning. For now, we chew on rue, oyster mushrooms,
avoid the pincher bugs who have made nests in manmade ecotones.
When the streetlights retreat, there are geckos
spawning amongst the weeds.

Mint

Grandma played me her garden song
during the shallow heat of springtime

She beat her palms against the soil
caressed the dirt-laced scrapes on my knees,
jewels of transcontinental sweat lined her bosom
as she hacked up furtive weeds

Granny licked her peeling sugarcane lips
They parted, and forth sprung an aria of flowers

There were whole land masses dropping from her hands
breathing soul into fragrant coriander and parsley
ballads of San Juan and Mississippi, West Africa
reconciled in Sunday dew-kissed grass

Look how the slender spines of lilac
bow to the sunflower's sullen crowns
just yards away, a squash blossom
swan song wanes toward summer

She sat in the cool shade, mint leaves whistling
her back creaking
like slave ships on salted ocean
she's found ways to harvest her own skin

Ripe like wild bananas
slow and deliberate

Ellery Akers

Rachel Carson

I think of the way she bent over tide pools at night:
a woman stooped in the dark with her flashlight
as if she were stepping into the lit harness of her work.

I think of the way she lay under the stars
because they were medicine:

Tumors near the collarbone.
Pain in her spine.
Radiation. Krebiozen.
Arthritis. Iritis.
Sightless for weeks.
Listening as her friend read a draft out loud.

Remembering the robin that fell dead from a branch.

I think of the pages of notes about pesticides—

I moan inside—and I wake in the night and cry out silently for Maine—

And then, more notes about pesticides.

I think of the way the moon glazed the water
when she crossed out words and wrote other words.

I think of the way she knew that eels slid from brook to brook
and then to the sea.

I'm in luck,
because brown is cheapest, she said,
when she bought a wig
to cover her bald head at the Senate.

I could never again
listen happily to a thrush song, she said,
if I had not done
all I could.

They called her *spinster.*
Alarmist.
Communist.

I think of the eagles who came back because of her.
I think of her open gaze. Her resolve.
Her refusal to turn away from the wreck.

Ruth Awad

Hunger

Imaginary, the value of the pound, and yet when it drops

like an apple rotted from its branch, my family may starve.

1,507 pounds to the dollar. What that means if you're not

an economist: a kilogram of meat is now a luxury. A line

huddles outside a Beirut bakery though the price of subsidized

bread is up again. The worst financial crisis in 150 years,

the World Bank says. And I don't see the story anywhere

here. In my house with its lights on. Where I choose to skip

meals. Once we were stitched together by food stamps.

Dirt poor, my mother describes it, though land is more valuable

than almost anything. America and its incongruent abundance:

fields of corn and the hungry in the streets. The cattle well fed.

Security guards in grocery stores. If you die from hunger, the spirit

goes searching for food and the wanting never stops. Hard to say

what you'd do to live. My father picked an apple from someone's

tree, was chased until he dropped it. If you steal an apple, it's a crime.

If you withhold an apple from someone who's hungry, it's not.

The Years of Water & Light

In the rowboat I tied her shoes.

           And the river cussed and spat.

Our feet swelled and our bellies begged.

           The end is never how you expect.

This is where I lose her:

           at the shoreline, in sweet water.

We fed wild dogs overripe applies and herring.

           My hands shine with hunger.

Her hair hung in willow boughs, mine in wild onion.

           I reel the small fish of time.

The end never happens and always happens.

           In winter we suet the trees. The cardinals arrive like snow.

I braid her willow hair. I tie her shoes once more.

           It is winter again. The birches like crooked combs.

Why are you crying?   *Why are you crying?*

           Begin but start with the end:

in spring she is pregnant. In summer she is not.

           The baby swims in every room.

See where our steps wet the hallway?

           That was when we were swept away.

Subhaga Crystal Bacon

Warming, Cooling; Wet, Dry: Burning Haibun

We can't keep up with the change in temperature. In the morning, the sun shines, and if you walk out into the hills facing south, drop into the ravines, it's too hot for your clothes. By afternoon, snow gathers over the mountains in foggy clouds in the west. The wind slices through cloth, skin, and applewood smoke flaps down from the roof. In the pearlized light, budding branches whip and shine like wizards' wands: chokecherry buds cluster at the ends of slender branches. Forsythia, too, burns golden at its tips. The grass on the barely thawed ground greens in spite of itself, drinks deep from the gone snow melted down into the earth. East, the sky emerges blue behind cumulus clouds that merge with mountaintop. Which is air, which is snow? What lives between them?

*

                change in temperature.   the sun
    the hills   the ravines,

                                    slices   cloth, skin,
and   smoke   pearl   light   branches
      wizards' wands: chokecherry   Forsythia
   burn   ground greens
        gone   sky emerges   cumulus
          mountaintop   air   What lives between   ?

*

                              sun
     hills   the ravines, /

                     pearlized light   branches

burn
      gone /
        mountain   air   is snow //

David Baker

Extinction

When you are gone they will read your footprints,
if they still read, as they might a poem about love—
wandering in circles, here and there obscured,
washed out in places by weather, sudden landslide.
Keep walking, pilgrim. This is your great tale.

Ned Balbo

A Spell for Lamentation and Renewal

Lamentation

For the quiet of the hazel
For the seed inside the acorn

For the fading of the bluebell
For the shadow of the fern

For the turning of the adder
For the wingbeat of the cygnet

For the tumbling of the otter
For the torn limb of the newt

For the wavering of willow
For the gathering of wrens

For the grasp of mistletoe
For the hazel's dangling catkins

For the dandelion's nectar
For the kingfisher's blue flash

For the cowslip's common hour
For the clearings marked by ash

For the brittle skin of beech tree
For the empty miles of pasture

For the steep ascent of ivy
For the silence of the future

Renewal

In the quiet of the hazel
In the blazing of the bluebell

In the acorn's buried secret
In the fossil print of fern

In the shedding of the adder
In the splashing of the otter

In the calm sleep of the cygnet
In the smooth skin of the newt

In the long stride of the heron
In the hazel's wealth of catkins

In the shelter of the willow
In the clasp of mistletoe

In the cowslip's golden hour
In its cluster and its nectar

In the kingfisher's brief flash
over clearings, over ash

In the vellum of the beech tree
In the timeless arc of ivy

In the burgeoning of pasture
In the promise of the future

— Written with words excised from abridged Oxford dictionaries

The Wolves of Chernobyl

The exclusion zone around the Chernobyl nuclear power plant
extends for a radius of nineteen miles.

At twenty below, the wolves forsake the forest's
infinite birches, padding over snow.
Habitable human settlements
cling to the zone's edge, snowbound. Then and now,

trefoil signs warn travelers not to pass.
Searching for prey that's scarce in winter's freeze,
the wolves move quietly. They're gone by day,
leaving their prints to trail past human boundaries,

back and forth. They scavenge in the dark.
Villagers at the zone's edge scavenge, too.
Displaced or very old, they gather mushrooms,
farm, and graze their cows—what can they do?

Whatever the soil contains, they have to eat.
Close to the epicenter of the zone—
past tracks and transport bridges, younger trees—
a "red forest" turned rust-red by radiation

lies bulldozed, pristine. A hunter, armed,
tracks down a wolf, its snow-prints filling in.
The night it happened, witnesses reported
colors in the sky they'd never seen—

ionized iridescence, a beam of blue . . .
Today, the wolves reclaim the land, and thrive.
A woman swings an ax beside a bonfire
in the snow. This winter, she'll survive,

as will the troops who dig up earthen trenches
in the red forest's dust: conscripts unsure
of why their armored vehicles stop here
where no one welcomes them, and wolves endure.

Stacey Balkun

The Water, the Truth, the Water

Located less than five hundred feet from the former site of the
Wynnewood Swim Club in Piscataway, New Jersey, is the chemical
pond used by Union Carbide during the active phase of plant operation.

I go only as far as I dare   a full-grown possum-girl
through the familiar neighborhood   past the NO TRESPASSING signs
behind the pool   a stream runs through and
collapsed razor wire squares the chemical pond   it's 2018 and backhoes
                                                                                    have torn at
my shiver   my urge to wade in   the earth   scraped   the residue stuck
to my insides   I can't rely on   memory
or ask my dead   the satellite maps   refresh
a thousand miles away   tomorrow I'll zoom close
to see the diving board sticking out   pale tongue lapping
the deep end   we count the steps   from swimming pool to waste pond
100 muddy paces between chlorine and acetone as   children   swam in
                                                                                    both and
the stream   my body plunging to the bottom
branches where I hang by   the strength of my storyteller tail
                          the map
                    makes it seem farther
I want to know why   I keep scouring
Nobody ever believed me   but the water never recedes

In the Forest

we were storied, we were mud, rooted

into branch, Adam-less, pond scum, we were

not abandoned, not *boys hunt, girls sew* but river

otters and acorns, we were boar hunters run wild

with electric charge, riding crop, we were

riot, rushing past the dropped fruit

we could sing poorly but loud, tangled hair

and chalked lungs, we were baptized

above radioactive dirt, we were bicycle chains,

daisy chains, grass stains, more than crumbs

left for birds: mammalian, marsupial, we could swing

from high on the highest branch to crack the surface of the creek

we did not dream of escape until we did, each tree a girl

who couldn't scream, our bones ringing like bells

Mildred Kinonco Barya

Cast Over Gorée Island

Hope absent from the Door—
last point of departure,
home to all they've known.

The child is exchanged for a
mirror, its mother a bottle of
rum, and the man a gun.

Atlantic sharks that wouldn't
eat every day or even choose
humans swallow samples.

Taste buds are forever
changed, millions of years
reversed; they grow fat
following ships.

Bodies that cross and land
meet a similar fate in trees,
attract buzzards and crows.

But why do clear skies like
Saint Kitts's bouncing off blue
waters make me sick?

Here where we are, snow drips
on our doorstep, falling like the
saddest note carrying our tune.

Janée J. Baugher

Andrew Wyeth's Footnotes to *Frosted Apples,* 1967

1. The tree trunk is a white-light against the solemn brown of the woods beyond.
2. Final apples of the season. Who has use for their cores?
3. Not every fruit is forbidden fruit but all fruit is miraculous.
4. *Fruit.*

> * Youth for eternity.
>
> † Fathers teach us what to do with our hands.
>
> ‡ Ink the sister red.
>
> § Dilute the colors for their motion.
>
> ¶ Ask for forgiveness.

5. A mighty wind and the trees are stripped of leaf and round.
6. While the world silences, I paint my family for our land.
7. Apples frosted winter.
8. A bare tree itself tells you nothing about its fecundity. Time determines whether it'll blossom.
9. "I have great faith in a seed." (Thoreau)
10. Here on this plane of wove paper, how to paint a mood cold and fleeting?
11. *Sometimes I think I'm not very artistic.*
12. Apples drop in evidence of Newton, travel down the hill, and into the bulbous trunk of a neighboring tree, which is where a gatherer stationed herself—see the half-full burlap bag? What that sack contains could be apples, but one should never be certain of anything.
13. At the base of the tree, apples rot.
14. You're not owed fruit even if you cultivate an orchard.
15. Nature needs no one.

Andrew Wyeth's Footnotes to *The Carry*, 2003

[1] "I have always been regretting that I was not as wise as the day I was born." (Thoreau)

[2] *Carry.*

      * A Maine portage.

      † Transition.

      ‡ To support, to conduct.

      § Temporary type of shallow.

[3] I slip into the woods for quiet, to be stupefied by it, but then I hear water.

[4] Water from up that slope, down and over rock-face, through the meadow.

[5] I sit at the confluence of streams and try to get how everything's conjoined. What gets caught in river gets carried by river. River's got a source, a wet mouth.

[6] I stand on the riverbed. I dip my hand into the current's force and then paint it as a white down-rock cascade crashing to foamy white.

[7] Its path of purpose and patronage is why I've come. I wait for it, for sometimes the connections aren't evident or timely, sometimes how we carry each other isn't clear.

[8] Painting river sounds isn't something I've yet mastered.

[9] Imagine a boat. Imagine a sunny day made cool by the forest canopy, made cacophonous by the thrashing river. Carried through, the journey made whole.

[10] Followed, this river will deposit me to sea.

[11] It's flow at the carry, before which I exist unchanged or changed.

Anna Lena Phillips Bell

Emerald

A charm for ash (Fraxinus *spp.*)

Deepening leaf-green: spring sun climbing summerald,
Causing sugars, calling out sugars, strengthening,
Pulling water, sipped from soil, up-and-overald,
Deepening leaf-green.

Seepen, sapwood, goldentire, emergenerald,
Groundwatern, leavy, windition, growind, treen,
Brighternally, spressively, nutrientire, goldenerald.

Shimmer, shake, outshine, new stems extenerald;
Rain from crown down bark to roots' beginning;
Opposite, live, inevitable—attenerald—
Deepening leaf-green.

Note: The emerald ash borer (*Agrilus planipennis*) was first found in
North America in 2002. The beetle is generally not fatal to ash species
(*Fraxinus* spp.), which it coevolved with, but since humans introduced
it to the continent—likely via wood used in packing and shipping—tens
of millions of ash trees, across thirty-six U.S. states and five Canadian
provinces, have died.

Jared Beloff

The Bird Collector

Last summer's pulse nudged the tide, noticeable as salt graining the sea-wall. But the mangroves are pulling back, their roots like frayed brooms holding on to detritus. Spoonbills, gangly and roseate, have already left Biscayne Bay for higher ground. Somehow this hasn't been registered as a fact we can grieve. It is my job to collect the dead that circle Miami's mirrored light: black- throated warblers lit by a night's shine, northern parulas searching out a distant home. Each bird crashes dreaming of a windowed horizon, not realizing the sea and its dotted green is already behind them. Everyone here is looking for more space and time. A group of warblers is called a confusion, spoonbills are called a bowl. I lay them out in lines like ruffled silver, a tide of feathers, a confusion of bodies, their mouths clattered open in search of food, a name lilting their small tongues. They stare out as if wondering which species is called a drawerful.

Ariana Benson

Black Pastoral

There is a kind of poetry in a turning that leaves
a body redder than before. Golden drupes ripen,
orchards flush rouge. Sweetness curls the blades
of leaves that once sprouted green. Fall confetti rains
red herrings in pretend surrender: showers of bleeding
white flags. Yes, even the trees play possum
when a cold force looms larger than they. They freeze,
mine stone from wood, statue themselves like deer.
Enter the fledgling buck. See him, just barely: a tawny smudge
blinking back at you through the landscape's static.
His molting crown: one shredded antler a tree in its own
visceral autumn, the other a felled trunk at rest
in the ashen grass. *Enter the Black boy.* See his boots leave
little coffin-prints in the ground—what lingers in the foam
of his wake. They stand together, this boy, this deer,
each a lone solstice removed from fawnhood, from his spring
-pink and summer-blushed self, the memories of whom live
only in the glossy black of the other's eyes. They reminisce
for a moment in unblinking silence. Then, see
the boy's tiny hands, dotted with birch-knot knuckles, his womb
-smooth palms split along umber fault lines, as they meet
to cradle the lost horn and turn it upright in the frost,
making sapling of skeleton. Now hear a distant whistling,
a herd of cocked rods dragging like fingernails over the shivering
ground, its goosebumped skin. See our subjects assume the position
of hibernation, of stagnant and threatless sleep, praying
they will awaken when the white recedes. They learned,
in leaving the red of their mothers, the danger of hound
-snouted men, who, upon cornering a creature dark
with life, ponder the taste of metal-peppered flesh.
They know to freeze, to still their limbs, wait for the melt,
for the trees to weep the winter out—the silent sobs a prelude
to the red, not of end, but of moss. Of possibility.

Love Poem in the Black Field

Chesapeake, Virginia, 1891

Listen. I did not mean to come to you empty
        -Handed. To be yet another who only takes.
My father taught me better than to milk dry
        What I cherish. I meant to bring you my fists
Full of wildflowers: buttercups and loosestrife.
        Aster and thistle wild as wind. I paid the man
At the riverbank—his cedarwood cart splintered
        By the brackish spray, his nailbeds stained
A deep blue that fades, like shoreline, into tan.
        I bought you a lush posy to hold
While we watch schooners troll the swamp.
        But darling, I've been an owned thing.
I've been the orphan calf, baying; been the birth
        -Damp hay cut and baled a few days before.
I know we keep livestock for meat and hides,
        Hens for their eggs—but is beauty enough
Reason to claim what once lived unpossessed?
        Please understand, I had to put them back
In the dirt. I plucked their seeds with my teeth,
        Spat them along the trail. Felt each one crush
Under the stone of my heel as I walked here, to you.
        I know I must sound mad. I hope I'm the kind
Of mad that makes you feel most whole.
        Think how, when we're sun-pruned and weary,
We'll stroll here, among the wayward blossoms.
        How right—to love in a field of our own making.

Sherwin Bitsui

from Dissolve

[A FIELD THAT SHIVERED WITH A THOUSAND CRANES]

A field that shivered with a thousand cranes
                    evaporates in someone else's backyard.

Gills sliced into the mountain's crest   resins hourly.

Televised vapor muzzles a hummingbird's gassed lungs.

A cliff line wavers
                under a table's August.

Shears jangle in the corral's black-and-white photograph.

In the trailer's hallway: the night's unveiled ankles.

Rented from a shepherd of doves
      we return   replenished with categories.

We are husbands to razed hillsides; wives to drowned bridges.

When interred in plexiglass: our origin *salinated*.

[ON LIMBS OF SLANTED LIGHT]

On limbs of slanted light
painted with my mind's skin color,
I step upon black braids,
oil-drenched, worming
from last month's orphaned mouth.

Winged with burning—
I ferry them
        from my filmed eyes, wheezing.

Scalp blood in my footprints—
my buckskin pouch filling
        with photographed sand.

No language but its rind
        crackling in the past tense.

Allen Braden

Inspiration

Not far from where a coyote led me
over the sparsely timbered hillside,
I found a feather held in the sagebrush
flanking an abandoned logging road.
I knew the pattern, its bars of tan
almost the color of parchment
or that coyote's pelt actually.
The feather of a great horned owl.
You could say the darker, narrower
scribbles curving toward the quill
suggest rows of silhouettes in flight.
You could say a lesson might exist
in the wind's subtle dispersal of dust
trickling through Sheepskull Gap,
estranging that feather from its wing.
All you really need to tell anyone
is how a single feather was poised
so the tip of the quill wrote on thin air.

Tina Mozelle Braziel

What the Creek Says

The creek says *littlehip hawthorn,*
      blackbanded darter, says *fiery skipper*
and *hearts a bustin' with love.*
      The creek says *pipsissewa* with a grin
widening from saying such.
      The creek claims in this beginning,
there is *pigtoe, fleabane, studfish,*
      and *yellow-shafted flicker.*
Words becoming petal and shell,
      words becoming feather and flesh.
The creek says say them with me,
      say *black redhorse,* say *indigo bunting,*
Eastern spadefoot, Alabama hogsucker.
      Say *oblong sedge borer* and *sassafras.*
Say them all here, call them into being.
      The creek suggests you hike while calling
devil's walking stick and *black racer.*
      The creek wants you to sit and watch
for the *slowpoke moth,* a *southern zigzag,*
      and a *false underwing.* The creek says
take a stroll and belt out *raccoon, fox,*
      and *belted kingfisher.* Then listen.
Call all the *warblers,* the *black-throated green,*
      the *yellow-rumped,* the *prairie,*
the *worm-eating,* call every last *warbler* into warbling.
      Come on in, the creek says,
meet the *Canoe Creek clubshell,*
      feel the cool of the *rainbow shiner,*
the *mimic shiner,* the *silverstripe shiner,*
      and the *largescale stone roller.*
The creek says say *Big Canoe*
      as you dip your oar, says
say *Creek* as you balance
      light as whisper on these waters.

Nickole Brown

A Prayer to Talk to Animals

Lord, I ain't asking to be the Beastmaster
gym-ripped in a jungle loincloth
or a Doctor Dolittle or even the expensive vet
down the street, that stethoscoped redhead,
her diamond ring big as a Cracker Jack toy.
All I want is for you to help me flip
off this lightbox and its scroll of dread, to rip
a tiny tear between this world and that, a slit
in the veil, Lord, one of those old-fashioned peeping
keyholes through which I can press my dumb
lips and speak. If you will, Lord, make me the teeth
hot in the mouth of a raccoon scraping
the junk I scraped from last night's plates,
make me the blue eye of that young crow cocked to
me—too selfish to even look up from the flash
of my damn phone. Oh, forgive me, Lord,
how human I've become, busy clicking
what I like, busy pushing
my cuticles back and back to expose
all ten pale, useless moons. Would you let me
tell your creatures how sorry
I am, let them know exactly
what we've done? Am I not an animal
too? If so, Lord, make me one again.
Give me back my dirty claws and blood-warm
horns, braid back those long-
frayed strands of every nerve tingling
with all I thought I had to do today.
Fork my tongue, Lord. There is a sorrow on the air
I taste but cannot name. I want to open
my mouth and know the exact
flavor of what's to come, I want to open
my mouth and sound a language
that calls all language home.

Collective Nouns for the Anthropocene

Say a *guillotine* of coal mines, a *phantom limb*
of peaks—all those headless mountains once called
home. Say a *jones* of cell phones, a *heart's burn*
of information, the flash and rush of us
measured in megabytes per second. And forget

spring—such a nostalgic word now—it's seventy
in February already and besides for years it's been
little more than *roadkill season*, all those newborns
mewling in bent grass, the milk-filled teats they wait for
meat-streaked across the street. Or say a *wonderment* of

children, at least those few still playing outside,
quickening Styrofoam cups with a writhing catch
of whatever insects and minnows are left to find.
Say a *blister* of news, another *throe* of tornadoes,
a heat rash spreading, slow-cooking

us all, a *dying nation* of amphibians that do,
in fact, jump when the red eye glowing
on a lab stove's burner is cranked up one slow
degree at a time, despite the myth a frog's too dumb
to know when boiling alive.

But what does it matter when the water's
rich with factory runoff, when you can jump all you want
but there's no way to get out of nowhere
else to go? Say a *click-through* of desperation,

a *comfort porn* of goats-in-pajama videos
and sneezing panda memes, a few seconds that pass
as joy with each clip. And because there are also
serious films to watch, understand
cats and dogs is no longer sufficient enough

metaphor, say instead a *hard rain of walrus:*

now that the ice they need is gone, watch how the herd
hauls up to a place they don't belong—a rocky precipice,
how cumbersome thousands wobble up and up
a jagged incline until it's too late, and like us,

they've stranded themselves with no room left
and can't back down. They crowd the ledge until
one by one they plummet over the side,
and as they fall, they find themselves confused—

falling being a thing walrus have never known
before, a thing they have no concept of at all,
at least not until humans got ahold
of this good earth. Yes,

one after another they fall, and like us,
they are not as afraid as they should be, and like us,
they are ignorant of laws of nature that apply to them.
And you might imagine their unintentional suicide

a grenade-confetti of blubber and ivory
sickening the shore, but no: most land
whole, their injuries internal, only a thin red trickle
from dead nose to dead eye to mark what happens
now that the world they knew has turned to melt.

I watched that footage, I did. I watched
all those walrus die and still—

still—I fired up my car again. I cranked up
the air. I stopped for a sip of sweet drink
in a plastic bottle and topped off
the tank. And still—if you were to ask me
what I was doing, I would tell you *not much,
just going about my day*. Because, yes—I'm sorry—

I too have used the word *murder* for a flock of crows,
that blessed oil-slick iridescence watching from above,
clacking to one another, assessing if I'm a benign
threat or something to actually fear. I too have used

the word *murder* when really it's just a word
for a *family* of those birds. I listen and listen
to their raspy *kraas*, a song of wet coal and hard
sun, ashamed they know the truth

of who I really am,
knowing the collective noun
we've given them
belongs wholly to us.

B. J. Buckley

Pronghorn Elegy

after Rilke's "Eighth Elegy"

On a clear night their eyes can see the rings
of Saturn in the vast openness of space
from the open vastness of prairie, their gaze
in utter stillness five-sixths of the horizon—
when they turn their heads they own the world:
sagebrush, bitterbrush, blue grama, rabbit
brush, prickly pear, wild oats, light and shadow, shades
of gigantic Pleistocene beasts
ten thousand years vanished behind them—
steppe lion, false cheetah, short-faced bear—millennia
unpursued, pronghorn still bunch
in selfish herds, the most vulnerable at the edges, they
are still fleeing, weightless swirl over waves of grass,
they are the wind, ridgeline skimmers light as birds,
breath and blood in a world of ghosts.

In the heat of this hellish summer they shimmer like
mirage in the drought-struck stubble, in fields of
withered wheat, of hollow-headed barley.
They cannot leap; before us, they never had
the need. Now every fence an *obstacle*
that blocks the path to freedom. To the last sparse
browse. To water. Does stand staring on the verges of
gravel roads to nurse their fawns, blanketed
in dust. Bucks pace miles of barbs and sheep panel.
None of them *free of death*. Some of us break locks on
headgates. Some of us cut wire in the dark.

Simmons Buntin

Desert Cottontail

Hopper but not hare, bunny but not jack, shit-
eater but not jackalope (that giver

of shit, launcher of tumbleweeds): cottontail
you zig through my thoughts like you zag

through the keen mind of my dog, the bone-
white shih tzu tracing your evening trail

& your riotous tail & so we both know
you are also on the mind of the rattler

who seeks your fur-lined nest, the coyote
who plays the opportunist (& why not:

he too steals the prickly pear's ruby meat)
& also the owls—great horned & barn—

not to mention, of course, the cats:
the yard's fat tabby you'd think couldn't catch

a whiskered thing but look at that bloody haul
& also the margay & bobcat, ocelot & mountain

lion & if the rumors are true the jaguar,
whose name means skull-crusher—

so back then to the canines: let's admit my pup
cannot compete with kit fox or gray fox or Mexican

gray wolf & also my flavorful friend
you scamper through the mind of red-tailed hawk

& Harris's hawk, Cooper's hawk & American kestrel
(ambitious, to be sure) & below them

the badger & the bear, weasel & raccoon, striped
skunk & hooded skunk & after all that

I coax my dog back as you sprint from every
talon & claw into the ravenous night.

Lauren Camp

I've started naming the landscape: sweet

I've started naming the landscape: sweet
      juniper coils, the sobbing

       olive, freezing crystals
that flower on barren ground.

      It's winter, a habitual bloom
           of wrestling wind, every
circumstance soiled by earth's
       revolution. I lean over
            to see what hasn't yet grown, what sin
    of snow, nerved branches.
To put this in perspective: never

      will I learn better
          how to follow the present
than the faint first sip of sumac. The aspens are accessible

to the sky, spines rising.
    And the full moon is coming up.

      The full moon pulls ten things
    from these graceless hours.

      The moon is still only one syllable.
The cat grabs another bird and leaves a wing.

Echinopsis Pachanoi

Tell me from your mouth what can be saved.
We cut apart the cactus with a sharp knife,
alcohol, mid-drift of thorn. The weather's turned
to a mist of heat. Awake, asleep.
The stems want only a bite of water
or rain aslant. Today's work
is dry weeds, a roadrunner slicking past yucca.
Sometimes when I feel betrayed, I need to lean
against the desert, to remember desire
isn't the end. Three-awn, kinnikinnick,
pine-drop seed stalks, the metronome
of sky, steady along.
Am I missing the answer: light
through its rotations?
Before I get old, I'll learn how it sings
nettle, scale, the spoon-breath
of dust-eddy, sip and remnant.
I will have seen a whole translucence.
The cactus insists on blooming. From joints,
eyeholes. Meaning, what splits from this
gives me the fortune to open
in welcome. I must want
what is empty. Map it, mention it, talk
all day. The month folds its tired self over me, clasps
without moving. I kneel
on the ground which keeps on
surviving. Above me wings with their rituals,
a sequence of hours, chance. All it takes
is summer again. Another morning.
What it hasn't been.

Wendy Taylor Carlisle

May We in This Time

In this time of misprision, in this time of plague and friction,
may we seek order in oil and unction. Boneless, indolent, errant us
let us call up the saints and martyrs: drowned, burned, thrown
to wild beasts, slain by a parent, by Vikings, or pagan Frisians
stabbed with iron pens, crucified, canonized, vanished,
or like Saint Bartholomew, stripped to muscle and vein, flayed
skin slung over one arm, and Saint Christina the Astonishing, flown up
from her coffin, come back from the dead to bring us hope.

In the two hours each night I hollow out from sleep, may I evoke
and consider them: the abbas and amas in their desert caves,
Saint Theresa, virgin warrior with the heart of a gladiator. Postulants
and monks who chant the hours. May I practice their intention,
livid and resistant, beseeching, believing in a prodigious
something, perhaps salvation, in the midst of larceny and disease.

Anders Carlson-Wee

Trash

Kneeling in a mix of good and bad
I sort by smell, never noticing
the garbage truck's approach,

not hearing, over the trainyard's
lonely horn, the scrape of forks
sliding into the dumpster's black

sleeves, until the machine
is lifting me like an offering
into the thick midsummer air.

Seconds later, after getting chewed
out by the driver, threatened
with arrest, and left behind

with the now-hollow dumpster,
I can't help but wonder what
would have happened to me if

I'd been taken away with the trash.
No doubt added to other masses
of trash, swept west by train car

and dumped on a bulk barge
bound for some poor other place
where they stuff the world's mecca

of waste, only to have some kid
not so different from me find
and dream up a use for my belt.

Emogene Cataldo

A question about procreation as the rivers dry

have you ever gutted a cantaloupe of its seeds?

or tossed a plump pit, thinking, *maybe*

I should plant this, maybe I should

make something grow

> but in what garden

> and what world

> what little bit of earth do you have

> on a fire escape

> in a country

> to make something begin

(it turns out—

Victoria Chang

The Ocean

The Ocean—died on August 21, 2017, when I didn't jump from the ship. Instead, I dragged the door shut and pulled up the safety latch. The water in my body wanted to pour into the ocean and I imagined myself being washed by the water, my body separating into the droplets it always was. I could feel the salt on my neck for days. A woman I once knew leapt out of a window to her death. The difference was she was being chased. Some scientists say the ocean is warming. Some say the ocean has hypoxic areas with no oxygen. Even water has hierarchy. A child's death is worse than a woman's death unless the woman who died was the mother of the child and the only parent. If the woman who died was the mother of an adult it is merely *a part of life*. If both mother and daughter die together, it is a *shame*. If a whole family dies, it is a *catastrophe*. What will we call a whole ocean's death? *Peace*.

Touching the Tree

How is it that trees
don't feel the way humans do?
The oldest tree is
five thousand years old, great storms
captured in its trunk.
A heart never grew inside
us. It was buried.
Its beat never meant to keep
time, just meant to keep distance.

Robin Chapman

That slant of sun

*There is no way of telling people that they are all walking around
shining like the sun.*
— THOMAS MERTON

Do the wavelengths reaching green leaves
shift as we tilt toward autumn, is it light
that tells the maples to bring out their reds,
their yellows, their anthocyanins—forget summers'
photoreceptors, go for the gold?

What cues our blackbirds, our grackles,
our geese into flocking? What orients them
to the south? And the high winds they ride—how
do they read the day of leave-taking,
the light, the weather, the route?

In this changing weather will the jet stream
still carry them home? And will they find
new winter grounds? Is it the low light that slows
the ripening of raspberries, the marigolds' blooms?
What slows our own steps, blinkers our vision?

What shimmer draws the grackles, dressed
in their blacks, toward their own green-gold auras,
all shining? And the bees, flying
toward the ultraviolet dots and dashes
of pollen pointing their way to the places

calling them in to the blossoms? How transformed
a landscape could we see?
Where does the light come from in each face
watching the fall world in its turning
to catch the last rays of the sun?

Teresa Mei Chuc

Mother of Waters, River of Nine Dragons

Dam construction on the Mekong River poses a serious threat to the region's economies and ecosystems.
— BRAHMA CHELLANEY, AUGUST 2, 2019

I.

Sông Mê Kông, flowing from the Tibetan Plateau
through China, Myanmar,
Laos, Thailand, Cambodia, Việt Nam
and into the country of my heart

where the wild rice grows
and the villagers live and have lived
for thousands of years,

II.

where the Irrawaddy dolphins,
the giant catfish and the softshell turtles swim,

where the sarus cranes feed
on insects, seeds, fish in the river reeds,
and open their majestic wings to take flight,

where the lilies and lotus bloom,
where our ancestors are alive,

III.

where the water buffalo bathe
their thousand-pound bodies
submerged in the river of my soul,
their heads on the water's surface,
curving horns pointing toward the sky,

where Sông Cửu Long,
River of Nine Dragons flows
through thick palm and green mangrove forests,
where the douc langur and white-cheeked gibbon exist,

and the salt- and freshwater mix,

I, your daughter, am forever connected to you
though thousands of miles away.

Chernobyl Necklace

The scar is a pink horizon, sunset at the ocean. Each tree
still standing in the Red Forest carries the story in its rings.
Blind birds sing, calling to their mates. Broken glass, a plastic
doll: the inanimate survive. How many more Aprils will
that day be remembered? On my body grow mushrooms
that could kill. Out of my heart runs a six-legged deer.

Anthony Cody

brd

stdnt sks

      hw s th flyng thng splld?

tchr sys

      ll th sft lttrs hv blwn ff

      spll brd

                    lk   brd

tchr tlls stry

      frst mnfst dstny

      th bffl wr hntd nd skltns stckd

      th ntv ppl wr pshd n slghtrd

      tk wht th y cn s

      thn crps plntd nd plntd nd plntd nd plntd

      thn dry nd ht nd dry nd cld nd dry nd ht

      thn rbbts nd rbbts nd rbbts

      thn mn clbbd ll th rbbts

      pld nd lghd

      vrythng brnd

      ll th ppl thrstd nd th lnd crckd

      brd jst lft bfr snrs nd snst

      brd dsspprd

      thn nsts mpty

stdnt sks

      wht hppnd t brd?

tchr sys

      brd sys n brnchs t prch nd crps cllps

      nd hrvsts nd n wrms s hngry

      brd sys   spk sky   spk   drk spk

ll thngs trnd psdwn

stdnt sks

                              thn blw

                              wy

nd trnds nd hrrcns nd wrs nd dss
nd nthng lvng

stdnt sks

dd brd knw?

tchr nswrs

brd knw   trd t spk
                    thrt splt

brd ndd wtr

stdnt sys

whts wtr?

Daniel Corrie

Wiregrass, Bluestem, Indian Grass, Palmetto, Ferns, Wildflowers, Blackberry, Gallberry, Longleaf Pine, the Sweep of Fire

i.

Awhile, I stood beside some land I burned
and heard fire's sound.

Beneath the pines, gallberry crackled black
where fire gleamed.

I closed my eyes and recognized the sound
seemed heavy rain.

By the firebreak, my eyes closed as
pines dreamed me there.

ii.

Dark depths of fireflies and stars will blink,
sparking through sleep.

In night's deep trance, Shiva will shiver bright
as shimmer's dance.

Night sees his shape twist, ripple, pour, veer, glare,
flare, rear, devour.

Stars follow stars into the starless dark,
in dreamlessness.

iii.

Through fleeting quests and meaninglessness,
days blaze a line.

Beneath the pines, I bore the driptorch down
the scar of earth.

I walked the firebreak and heard flames call
as rain's loud fall.

When grasses sprouted back from blackened earth,
pines dreamed my path.

Britney Corrigan

The Strip Mall Changes Its Mind

At first, it took comfort in the scents from Body Beyond:
floral powders and cinnamon lotions mingled in the stuffy dim.

It watched over so many unfooted shoes. Bright dresses called out
in bold prints to suits in the dry cleaner's rack, still rows of ghosts.

Then the grief set in, the conveyer belt of Sushi Town twisted
like an empty gut. Its capillaries of people gone, quiet at the heart.

Undone, it hardly noticed windows shattering, walls crumbling
as trees limbed their way in. Sunlight on every rain-warped floor.

Missing the humans with their electric bodies, wires and pipes
spilled out between unmoved beams. Tireless beaks bored holes

in everything. But the moss was so soft. It made the unframing
bearable. Signs unlatched, bedded down in tendrilled leaves.

When the fox moved in, birthed two russet kits in a thicketed
shopping cart, wind like a breath, a sigh, rose past the splintered

rafters, the unlit lights. And so it happened: the forgetting. Painless,
its tender reclaiming. Dangling ceiling tiles sloppy with stars.

Anthropocene Blessing: California Condor

King of birds, you of the nine-foot wingspan,
you who glide for hours on currents of air
without a single beat, thousands of feet above
the leaden earth. Scavenger ancestor, only
surviving member of your genus, longest-lived.
May you feast on the flesh of the dead
as you toss their spirits up to the sky. May
the carrion ghosts look down upon your
unplumaged head, your black-feathered,
sacred form, and be healed of all that stalked
them in this world. May you be not poisoned
by our buckshot, seething in each carcass
we leave behind. May you outgrow our
captivity to hatch your single eggs in mountain
cliff caves, giant redwood trees. New World
vulture, may your bulbous, wrinkled visage
remember how you soared over mammoths.
May you be revered as virtuous, as rising back
from the brink, as gathering your flock around
the fallen. May you take death in your mouth
and find it sweet, find that it sustains.

jason b. crawford

A Double Sonnet for the River

and because this is a poem about joy, it too must have a river flowing
from its greedy jaws. i have only learned how to speak about joy
as an offering to a god i will never understand. i once watched a fire
hydrant open its locked-turned throat and flood the city in what
i mistook to be the fresh smell of the thornapple; and because
of my own instinct, i expected a school of children, wide in their grins
and teeth fencing about their gums, to swim toward the cracked
basin, searching for salvation, cooling their mouths with the sharp taste
of nickel, and because I am reminded of my childhood, chasing a spitting
sprinkler head in my front yard or of the trips to the houghton lake
that held shores of loose sand that could swallow a child whole but we chose
to stomach the dirt gripped at our feet, treading the deepest palm of the
shallow end while our parents watched from the beach just as how I now
watch these children choosing to defy the act of drowning; typical how
they sought what once killed us, how it is now ailing their dry tongues.

and because this is a poem
about joy, i trust the river
to hold me longer
than could the ocean's
open barrelled hands.
i trust no god like i do
my own people,
if i am to die, let it be
in the presence
of the ones that
loved me most, let me drown
in their mouths and
continue flowing
through their veins

Laura Da'

An Unknowable Creator Departs the Talking Fields

At the neck of Samish Island a chestnut draft horse is freed
of his stays. He turns his head to nuzzle patches of sweat
where the leather just sat. The torte with blackberries and lemon
rind crackles between my teeth. Flycatchers depart and the loons
return wafting over the waterline with pale ringed necks
and red eyes. I walk a spit of the Skagit estuary heedless
of the hunting safety zone and season. Signs warn me
I may be inundated with the tide. Down a long trail colonnaded
by dense velvet clubs of cattails: oystercatchers prance
in the mud flats, yellow mouth eagle on the snag. The air
takes on thick licks of salt and I am walking a mosaic
surface through the sea water, dun cut with slim channels.
The clot of swallows streaming from the cornfield miles inland
arrow to a delicate smear of grime on the flat gray horizon
of my backward glance. Gull calls warble with eerie resonance
as the sea bends my legs and takes me to the chest
holding my arms to my sides. My eyes go bloodshot and I dive.

The Meadow Views: Sword and Symbolic History

When skirted by a river's confluence,
    a mountain range, or other natural boundary,
    a meadow is an optimal gathering place; lush cradle
    with its own established treaty rites
    of diplomacy and abundance.

The word *meadow*'s English etymology
    precedes the dissolution of the monasteries
    and the routine cadastral measurement of land.
    So it leaves a soft cast in the throat,
    a taste of Edenic green in its syllables.

Meadow is a woven basket
    pressed under epochal currents,
    reaping old arrows of hunger,
    sifting hard mineral traces of appetite.

A gang of fifty elk saunter
    the leeward edge as one body;
    the last of the light hemming
    across mountain crowns.

The elk press, slow and deliberate,
    until the meadow is defined,
    a rippling frontier
    between their calves
    hidden in the marsh grass
    and me, walking slowly backward,
    pulses thudding across
    the ridges of my fists.

To conceptualize the words
    of faith, I was taught to
    hold a phantom sword
    in my hand and study the verses
    by its points.

An allegory of conquest
      so simple a child
      can understand it.
      Is there a sin to avoid?
      Is there a promise to believe?
      Is there an example to follow?
      Is there a command to obey?

Many perceive heaven
      in the form of a meadow. The path of righteousness
      is carpeted with violet flowers. The open
      field symbolizes doctrine; faith is grasses.

I am too close, and have forgotten
      that I am a stranger here.
      Ochre ripples of hair
      crest on the nearest elk.

The crown of my head
      is the blade tip pointing
      to the dark opal of sky:
      What can be inferred about the divine?

Aidan Daniel

Virginia Possum Rages

*(she is unhopeful; hurt, quickly fading; found on the roadside,
heaving so softly)*

do not remember me like this/ remember each fine hair of all my
    promise/ when

possibility torrented around me/ remember me fast enough/ to fight my
    clouded eyes/

when no one could get close enough/ so all they called me was animal/ a
    specter a vision

in white/ remember the tonic of my million teeth grinding/ to
    antivenom any viper

threatening me/ remember nothing of me now/ loose and ungathered/
    ash after/ a wild

fire/ rather me with my dozen beloveds/ cargo of babies strung over my
    bones/

remember my womb/ another dimension/ my pouch a practical bull's-
    eye of lifegiving/

remember anything/ moon of my ear/ apple of my toes/ even better
    remember/ I just

play at death/ remember/ how I make it a joke

Noah Davis

Poem Sewn into My Hunting Jacket

When I say I am going to kill a deer on the mountain,
  I mean I want our daughter to have the strength to jump fences,
and when she doesn't come home at night we will know to find her
  in the neighbor's garden.

When I say we will know to find her in the neighbor's garden,
  I mean we will not worry about her in strangers' houses.
Because while she grew in you, I carried a deer down
  from the mountain, then fed you that deer so she
could be woven with the folding knowledge of the woods,
  which is always unfolding.

When I say we find her in the neighbor's garden,
  I mean she has the strength to jump fences,
and when I am weak with age, she will walk into the folding
  woods and kill a deer on the mountain.

Todd Davis

Apostate

Beneath a new moon I enter the vast and stoneless field,
feet bared to tilled soil where the very first rocks should be,
those stones who cried out and allowed trees to sprout
between them, roots holding. This was before the coming
of my grandfather and his grandfather who cleared a footpath
in the forest, a field owned and increasing on either side
of the path, which now is a road, and in that field with each plowing
stones unearthed, dragged to the far side with the help
of horses and mules, oxen oaring the weight of a stoneboat,
and there stacked, resting one upon another, exposed
as if in warning, no longer warmed by earth and now named *wall*,
and I do not know how long it will take to undo this doing,
but I begin with a single stone, carrying it to the field's center,
and there, like a seed, burying, then gathering another, disassembling
that wall, weight burning my back, planting rock after rock, making
impossible the plow's work, and with the aid of vireo
and thrush, warbler and wren, with the mouths and bowels
of so many animals, who just by eating and shitting plant
a new world: fences brought down, barriers returned to earth,
furrows forgotten, and a forest I will never see
already growing.

Lucille Lang Day

Lost Languages

It isn't just Hittite, Trojan, and Sumerian,
or even Mohegan, Yana, and Natchez,
all long gone, but also the hundreds
that have slipped away since 1950,
while the last Madeiran large white butterfly
flickered among the trees of the laurisilva,
the last West African black rhino
ran across the savannah, chased by poachers
after its horn, coveted as an aphrodisiac in
China, and the last Javan tiger, stripes rippling,
was poisoned, its forest habitat cleared for rice.

Lucille Roubedeaux, last surviving speaker
of the Osage language in Oklahoma,
died in 2005; Marie Smith Jones,
last speaker of Eyak, died in Alaska in 2008.

Biologists say ninety-nine point nine percent of
all species that ever existed are now extinct.
Perhaps the same is true of languages.
Who knows what Cro-Magnons said
to one another in sickness, love, or fear?
Now so many ways of dreaming and perceiving
are disappearing, but as Mojave, Comanche,
Bolo, and Beezen slip away, so do salmon,
salamanders, rainforests, and redwoods,
and even the speakers of English, Russian,
and Chinese become one with the red wolf,
mongoose, numbat, and tarsier in their fate.

Janine DeBaise

Woven

Roone's voice
leads me into the garden I carry inside of myself.
Past stone walls, cornfields, a cave of red clay. I swallow
seeds to fill myself with sunflower light.
Spirit guides ripple
through this circle of women. Flicker of feather
and breath. We thank sky and earth. Butterflies carry pollen
from wrist to wrist. We breathe smoke of sage and sweetgrass.
We carry earth
under our fingernails. We grow hemlock and
hostas, simmer fragrance over flame. We wear
essential oils, dishwater suds, poison ivy rash.
We stand safe
inside columns of light, touched by translucent cascade
of sparkle. We are woven together in this circle of shining,
elbow to elbow, our feet on the ground, rooted and strong.
We ask blessings
from twittering birds, cars humming past, kids playing
in the street, the pine tree who rubs her branches
against porch and window, against sky.
We give ourselves
to violet sunset fire. We grow flowers over scars, plant seeds
into soft spots that ache. We leave this earth to return
to this earth to find that we are made of earth. Oil and dirt.
We latch
our gates, helping each other lock tight
our dreams, our inner gardens, our blooming.
When you are ready, Roone says,
open your eyes.

Natalie Diaz

The First Water Is the Body

The Colorado River is the most endangered river in the United States—
also, it is a part of my body.

I carry a river. It is who I am: 'Aha Makav. This is not metaphor.

When a Mojave says, *Inyech 'Aha Makavch ithuum*, we are saying our
name. We are telling a story of our existence. *The river runs through the
middle of my body.*

So far, I have said the word *river* in every stanza. I don't want to waste
water. I must preserve the river in my body.
In future stanzas, I will try to be more conservative.

↠

The Spanish called us *Mojave. Colorado*, the name they gave our river
because it was silt-red-thick.

Natives have been called *red* forever. I have never met a red Native,
not even on my reservation, not even at the National Museum of the
American Indian, not even at the largest powwow in Parker, Arizona.

I live in the desert along a dammed blue river. The only red people I've
seen are white tourists sunburned after staying out on the water too long.

↞

'Aha Makav is the true name of our people, given to us by our Creator
who loosed the river from the earth and built it into our living bodies.

Translated into English, *'Aha Makav* means *the river runs through the
middle of our body, the same way it runs through the middle of our land.*

This is a poor translation, like all translations.

In American imaginations, the logic of this image will lend itself to
surrealism or magical realism—

..ericans prefer a magical red Indian, or a shaman, or a fake Indian in a red dress, over a real Native. Even a real Native carrying the dangerous and heavy blues of a river in her body.

What threatens white people is often dismissed as myth. I have never been true in America. America is my myth.

→

Jacques Derrida says, *Every text remains in mourning until it is translated.*

When Mojaves say the word for *tears*, we return to our word for *river*, as if our river were flowing from our eyes. *A great weeping* is how you might translate it. Or *a river of grief*.

But who is this translation for and will they come to my language's four-night funeral to grieve what has been lost in my efforts at translation? When they have drunk dry my river will they join the mourning procession across our bleached desert?

The word for *drought* is different across many languages and lands. The ache of thirst, though, translates to all bodies along the same paths—the tongue, the throat, the kidneys. No matter what language you speak, no matter the color of your skin.

←

We carry the river, its body of water, in our body.

I do not mean to imply a visual relationship. Such as: a Native woman on her knees holding a box of Land O' Lakes butter whose label has a picture of a Native woman on her knees holding a box of Land O' Lakes butter whose label has a picture of a Native woman on her knees . . .

We carry the river, its body of water, in our body. I do not mean to invoke the Droste effect—this is not a picture of a river within a picture of a river.

I mean *river* as a verb. A happening. It is moving within me right now.

→

This is not juxtaposition. Body and water are not *two unlike things*—they are more than *close together* or *side by side*. They are *same*—body, being, energy, prayer, current, motion, medicine.

The body is beyond six senses. Is sensual. An ecstatic state of energy, always on the verge of praying, or entering any river of movement.

Energy is a moving river moving my moving body.

←

In Mojave thinking, body and land are the same. The words are
separated only by the letters 'ii and 'a: 'iimat for body, 'amat for land.
In conversation, we often use a shortened form for each: *mat-*. Unless
you know the context of a conversation, you might not know if we are
speaking about our body or our land. You might not know which has
been injured, which is remembering, which is alive, which was dreamed,
which needs care. You might not know we mean both.

If I say, *My river is disappearing*, do I also mean, *My people are
disappearing*?

→

How can I translate—not in words but in belief—that a river is a body, as
alive as you or I, that there can be no life without it?

←

John Berger wrote, *True translation is not a binary affair between two
languages but a triangular affair. The third point of the triangle being
what lay behind the words of the original text before it was written. True
translation demands a return to the pre-verbal.*

Between the English translation I offered, and the urgency I felt typing
'Aha Makav in the lines above, is not the point where this story ends or
begins.

We must go to the place before those two points—we must go to the third
place that is the river.

We must go to the point of the lance entering the earth, and the river
becoming the first body bursting from earth's clay body into my sudden
body. We must submerge, come under, beneath those once warm red
waters now channeled blue and cool, the current's endless yards of
emerald silk wrapping the body and moving it, swift enough to take life
or give it.

We must go until we smell the black root-wet anchoring the river's mud
banks. We must go beyond beyond to a place where we have never been
the center, where there is no center—beyond, toward what does not need
us yet makes us.

→

What is this third point, this place that breaks a surface, if not the deep-cut and crooked bone bed where the Colorado River runs—a one-thousand-four-hundred-and-fifty-mile thirst—into and through a body?

Berger called it the *pre-verbal*. *Pre-verbal* as in the body when the body was more than body. Before it could name itself *body* and be limited, bordered by the space *body* indicated.

Pre-verbal is the place where the body was yet a green-blue energy greening, greened and bluing the stone, red and floodwater, the razorback fish, the beetle, and the cottonwoods' and willows' shaded shadows.

Pre-verbal was when the body was more than a body and possible.

One of its possibilities was to hold a river within it.

←

A river is a body of water. It has a foot, an elbow, a mouth. It runs. It lies in a bed. It can make you good. It has a head. It remembers everything.

→

If I was created to hold the Colorado River, to carry its rushing inside me, if the very shape of my throat, of my thighs is for wetness, how can I say who I am if the river is gone?

What does 'Aha Makav mean if the river is emptied to the skeleton of its fish and the miniature sand dunes of its dry silten beds?

If the river is a ghost, am I?

Unsoothable thirst is one type of haunting.

←

A phrase popular or more known to non-Natives during the Standing Rock encampment was, *Water is the first medicine*. It is true.

Where I come from we cleanse ourselves in the river. I mean: *The water makes us strong* and able to move forward into what is set before us to do with good energy.

We cannot live good, we cannot live at all, without water.

If we poison and use up our water, how will we clean our wounds and our wrongs? How will we wash away what we must leave behind us? How will we make ourselves new?

→→

To thirst and to drink is how one knows they are alive and grateful.

To thirst and then not drink is . . .

←←

If your builder could place a small red bird in your chest to beat as your heart, is it so hard for you to picture the blue river hurtling inside the slow muscled curves of my long body? Is it too difficult to believe it is as sacred as a breath or a star or a sidewinder or your own mother or your beloveds?

If I could convince you, would our brown bodies and our blue rivers be more loved and less ruined?

The Whanganui River in New Zealand now has the same legal rights of a human being. In India, the Ganges and Yamuna Rivers now have the same legal status of a human being. Slovenia's constitution now declares access to clean drinking water to be a national human right. While in the United States, we are teargassing and rubber-bulleting and kenneling Natives trying to protect their water from pollution and contamination at Standing Rock in North Dakota. We have yet to discover what the effects of lead-contaminated water will be on the children of Flint, Michigan, who have been drinking it for years.

→→

America is a land of bad math and science. The Right believes Rapture will save them from the violence they are delivering upon the earth and water; the Left believes technology, the same technology wrecking the earth and water, will save them from the wreckage or help them build a new world on Mars.

←←

We think of our bodies as being all that we are: *I am my body*. This thinking helps us disrespect water, air, land, one another. But water is not external from our body, our self.

My Elder says, *Cut off your ear, and you will live. Cut off your hand, you will live. Cut off your leg, you can still live. Cut off our water, we will not live more than a week.*

The water we drink, like the air we breathe, is not a part of our body but is our body. What we do to one—to the body, to the water—we do to the other.

→→

Toni Morrison writes, *All water has a perfect memory and is forever trying to get back to where it was.* Back to the body of earth, of flesh, back to the mouth, the throat, back to the womb, back to the heart, to its blood, back to our grief, back back back.

Will we remember from where we've come? The water.

And once remembered, will we return to that first water, and in doing so return to ourselves, to each other?

Do you think the water will forget what we have done, what we continue to do?

LaTasha N. Nevada Diggs

ᎤᏪᏴᎢ uweyvi is Tsalagi for river

victorian . perhAps . s ou th west . call It . medi terRa ne an .
return to tAr hee L . post-co lon i aL . pine & sweet gum .
detail e d stuc co . a creek . uweYv . a central cOurtyard .
a bUtler's paNtry .
        not far . a riv Er . meandering . black
wa t er riv Er . or a tribu ta ry of a mud Dy black m ean de r ing
ri ver . bea vers . a big muTt bla ck of a H oun d . w/ a clay til E
roof . fr on t gAbles . a mutt n ot allow ed in side . all n ew
fur ni ture . back to kakalak . y river fat w/ fIsh . great blue heron &
c oo ters . bR ush ed walls . sand . maYbe catfish grandma
caught ? yOur chickens your mUtt watches

Michael Dowdy

Blast Fragments

Mountain man, what do you need of life beyond your hills?
— JAMES STILL

The mountain stirs, a slug on quaaludes. Like basalt or beeswax, ridges slide.
Ghost of glacier, shade from a globe of crags. A sliver of haunting moon, sentry
of laurel thicket, dares the strip mine and dragline, spectral euphemism and sad
country song—come, bare your coffin rivets.

    There, dominion of root salve, lichen compass, dragonfly wing.
      A toddler's soles swivel in moss and limestone, spring-fed, leap giddy.
      At her heels, blast fragments from her old man's mountainsick jones.

Mountain as verb.   I'll sow azalea and huckleberry.
Mountain as mending thread.   I'll weave a path through knotty pine.
Mountain as force field, brimstone, curse and spell.   I'll bark, star-drenched,
                                            trembling.
Mountain as rubble museum, please visit.   I'll plant a ridge on a pinhead.
Mountain as collateral damage, market force, fossil.   I'll harvest air from
                                          the arid hills.

Planet otherwise, orbit my daughter's woods, her maple shine and bramble
grin. Tow her ark through backfill bones, dodging shoals of stump and copper
wire, fording currents of opioid and not a chance, nope. Glance anywhere here—
mountain man dripping dynamite rain. Mountain, man—a stake driven in the
surveyor's prey splinters his oaken rib.

Kendall Dunkelberg

The intergalactic traveler in springtime

It is always a surprise, this renewal of green shoots
in spring, the explosion of cherry blossoms and daffodils,
snakes, bees, and worms emerging from hibernation.
Surely there are other planets that spin on a tilted axis,
surely all heavenly bodies maintain some cycle of seasons,
fast or slow, changing in an instant or ebbing and flowing
over eons, and yet the profusion of springtime never
ceases to amaze and remind of the delicate balance, the
equilibrium sustaining the water cycle, weather patterns,
migrating birds, seeds sprouting, gardens and fields
to provide sustenance, even the excesses of springtime,
the buzzing of insects, the profusion of pollen, earthlings
with hay fever and March Madness, which only a few degrees
warmer or colder will throw completely out of whack.

The intergalactic traveler tells it like it is

We've seen it all before, those of us who roam the galaxies,
whether on the worlds we've abandoned or in the screams
we pick up in electromagnetic radiation. First we notice
the hubris and the hedonism, a species in love with its own
inventions, the narcissism and the focus on power. Then
comes their dawning realization, the denials, the unfettered
procreation, the utter disregard for every other life-form
in their ecosystem. Here, it manifests in wanton emissions
of carbon dioxide and other greenhouse gases, elsewhere
it may be silicon or nitrogen or undiscovered substances.
Yet in every instance there is blindness, there is delusion,
thinking only in the present, which is nearly always fatal,
though now and then, we land on a world teetering on
the tipping point, edging closer to a precipice, with barely
any time to open its eyes and correct course. Governments
are ponderous institutions, cautious and without a conscience.
Businesses are driven blindly by the bottom line. Sometimes
there is a child, sometimes a whole generation who pleads
for its future. Sometimes, though rarely, others even listen.

Iris Jamahl Dunkle

Black Blizzard

Roads without air.   Dust blooms.   The people pulse

around what is broken   nervous as gnats: as horse flies

that touch down then fly back up fast   for fear of being crushed

fields gone fallow   gone grave

under weight of another's life   topsoil

lifted from another far-off farm

No seed   takes   sprouts   finds light

Everything buried   in the dugout of now.

But the people   can still see it   the time before

thin as scrim   penciled in   over the dead land:

the dense sway   of six-foot-tall prairie grass

Then, the stalks of broom corn whistling wind

The tiny green curls of winter wheat

Disaster, a Reckoning

1. Disaster follows: Oklahoma to
2. California feral as a starved dog
3. that begs at the mouth of our door.
4. We always soften. Set out scraps. Huddle
5. under collapsed rooves, dodge the snakes of downed
6. wires. We wade through swollen rivers. We
7. dig out of anything. We silver boat.
8. We mask and back-burn. We can hold our breath
9. until our lungs bloom like pink peonies.
10. No one can tell our story. Get it right.
11. Ghost voices braided with living voices.
12. None of us afraid to eat what rots on
13. the ground. In fact, we get drunk off what it
14. distills: The sticky sweet truths you forgot.

Thomas Dunn

It was raining

It was raining all last night as it had yesterday as it did
the day before, the creek is foaming and when morning came it wasn't

raining anymore, so stumbling out into the green across the bridge,
'round a bend crossing more of the same water, letting

my eyes slope the tree line waving back stirring wind, I fold
at the spot; the moss-cracked steps, the ivy-laced

chateau, those soft pads of running shoes scuffing trails
matching the rhythms of jackhammers, table salt, forklifts

a   fuchsia   rose   sun   spotlight—

when someone asks what a poem does in the face of iron rain
bursting everything. Bright waves and birdcalls; when some-

one asks what's gained from a poem only about the things any-
one can see on a walk mapping routes up Potrero Hill sketching

the same steps again tomorrow—I pause to say:

every-
          -thing

Teresa Dzieglewicz

Baking Bread as Oceti Sakowin Is Raided

I.

Nobody stands at North Gate anymore,
        when bulldozers lumber the slope, score
                the dirt with their teeth, scatter
men who slash tipis in the wet earth
                     where we once lived.

Winona's kitchen,
        the tent where the kids donned rubber gloves
                ladled soup into hundreds of bowls,
crumples like a foal in the snow.

The sheriff calls this *victory*
        I am very happy to say that we finally introduced
                     rule of law in the Oceti camp,

and I am not there.
        I don't want to tell you this,
                but I am leaning against my stove
                     in Saint Louis, clutching a recipe's flimsy page,
                     written in black and white, as the blurry window of my computer
                     streams Oceti in from the edge of my counter.
I am just a woman whose back will not support her,
        in a city that hides its water
                behind high-voltage lines and highway,
starburst windows of forgotten factories.

The bulldozers power
        toward the Cannonball, river I slept beside,
                churn the earth and the roots
    of each plant as central heat pumps
                     like an old heart through my house.

2.

I used to trust the words
        that were placed on my tongue.
            I called the river "Missouri"
but learned no language
        for the dams, redirecting the water,
            holding back the stories
                of the silt and the clay.
I never learned of the children
        who were taken from its side. I never learned why
            I was taught to sing
                "This land is my land."

3.

The county commissioner says,
        he's *proud* the camp was cleared
            without any major injuries
    and I remove a glass measuring cup from my shelf.
Travis's plywood home, where he practiced
        the songs he would sing with the kids,
            the home he built with his hands, spray-painted,
                "We are unarmed," erupts into flames.
    I unfold the origami of the flour's
        silent mouth. The bulldozers turn and shred
            haybales that kept our tipis warm in the wind, yank
                the foundation from Tonia's wigwam,
    where Shaylena and Shawness
        last hugged me goodbye. The bag coughs
flour like dandelion seed, and I cannot
            come clean of it: coating my fingers white, wedged
white between the threads of my sweater,
            burrowed white
in the split wood of my counter.

On the screen, assault rifles
        push the last few people to the river.

4.

Some days, I lean against my sink,
     feeling the grinding in my spine and I am ashamed
          to say, that some small piece of me wishes I could close
            this window, simply follow the directions
               that have been written so clearly before me,
            let my world be the chipped white of my cabinets
                 the shift of the pots and pans above my head,
            forget I ever lived beside a river.

But the Missouri and the Mississippi
          become one and reach me, even here,
each time I turn my tap.
When the edges of the Cannonball overflow,
     touch the places along the riverbank
          where we sought sticks for drums,
    and studied the plants and sat in circles and sang,
            the water runs here.
     Every day, I brush my teeth with Oceti,
Every day, I wash my clothes with Oceti,
     Every day, it is Oceti that fills my glass.

5.

On the feed, the soldiers are chasing Eric
     who made tea for our coughs,
dipping into jars of marshmallow root
     and ginger and osha. Once he measured herbs
        with the kids, as I measure my water
     to the line, stir until strands of gluten begin to form.
     The camera bucks and I see only a river of sky
            and Eric is screaming.

6.

The governor says he is glad
     the efforts have gone so *smoothly*
        and, one-by-one, each feed blinks out.

7.

What we built is now just mud and sleet,
      ash and firewood, broken
            by bulldozer chains. Still, I see

the Sacred Fire in the summer, Frankie
      braiding my hair in the food line,
            Wolf and Junior grass dancing
      in the firelight. I don't know

when the pipeline will run
      beneath the river, when the water will brush
    its strange plastic tubes before it reaches our lips.
            I don't know if this bread will ever rise or
      when or where

the first oil will leak.
      But I am learning something small of how
            to see a river: to see the drowning hidden
               beneath the water, and see, also, the kids on the bank
covered in temporary tattoos, hair spiked from days
          of swimming. They are praying
            for the construction workers
Help them understand, their kids drink water too.
Tobacco sprinkles from their fingers,
        is taken in the breath of the current.

Martín Espada

Love Song of the Galápagos Tortoise

I am Lonesome George, the last Galápagos tortoise of Pinta Island.
I see Darwin's hairy face on T-shirts and hats, backpacks and mugs.
I see the statues. I can read the history books if someone turns the pages.

I remember Darwin. I was there the day he landed in the ship named
for a dog with floppy ears. He tried to lift me up and strained his groin.
He climbed on my saddleback shell and tried to ride me, giggling like
a boy on a birthday pony. He slipped off and rolled over in the surf,
spitting sand. He watched me plod around in search of cactus to crunch,
timing me with a pocket watch. He yelled in my ear to see if I was deaf,
and I hissed in his face. He invited my tortoise brothers and sisters
to board the *Beagle*. The crew hauled them up the gangplank as guests
of honor. Darwin noted in his journal: *Young tortoises make excellent soup.*
Like the pirates and the whalers, the naturalists licked their spoons,
soup in their beards, toasting the voyage with glasses of our urine.

I am Lonesome George. I crane my leathery neck and hiss at everyone.
I tuck my head inside my shell. You call and call my name till I peek out.
I am a creature of the tropics who curses the icebergs of December.
I groan about my gut, intimidating the curious with a drumroll of flatulence.
You feed me the cactus of Pinta Island and pizza from the Jersey Shore.
I am afraid of the toaster and dream of Darwin's beard caught in its coils.
You are afraid of nothing, as you make waffles jump from the glowing machine.
I plod down the road as cars honk behind me, seafarers hungry for soup.
You let me steer the car, even though the world is blurry and you yell
in my ear when the other cars cruise like pirate ships through stop signs.

I will hiss at the next TV reporter who calls me Lonesome George. This world
teems with pirates, whalers and naturalists on parade, waving their spoons
in the air, craving the delicacy of buttery tortoise flesh, but now I crane
my neck to croak the love song of the Galápagos tortoise for you, and you
swear I am your Frank Sinatra, I am your Sam Cooke, I sing better than Darwin.

Michelle Bonczek Evory

By root, by petal, by sword

They grew on roadsides, first in bunches
     like families, where asphalt hinged on
plain. Some claimed they had to be seeded
     by human will, their placement too perfect,

too symmetrical to be random, but
     in the deepest sense, they were wild,
wild in their perfume, intoxicating
     in their rouge electrifying
synapses of passersby who'd swoon
     their cars, unclasp seatbelts and rip them out—

mothers from root to be resettled into
     soil, showcased in pots glazed
with the colors of Mexico, Honduras, Brazil,
     other countries where people danced
and sang in the streets, men by stem

     wrapped in bright paper, presented in sheaths
like swords to the women they loved, children
     petal by petal to crush and darken
in their endlessly damp hands.

     They grew, they grew. Single, paired.
Widowed. Nobody could decide
     what to name them. For to name them
was to lose them, a lack tongued
     into tragedy because their extinction,

like all of ours, allowed them to live on
     as absence, translucent in the imaginations
of those who could never keep them alive,
     and by those, I mean we who tried.

Alyson Favilla

Bullfrog

I've swallowed a bowl
      of air.
I'm washing my insides
      with music.
I do this just for you:
      resonate
with the mellow slap
      of your feet.

I'm coaching
      the tight-lipped flowers,
bellowing under
      your window
a jukebox
      of desperation
made entirely
      of noise.

O, O lovely one,
      look,
I'm terrestrial now
      I've perfected
a thousand
      swollen imitations
of the ripe and ever-
      loving moon.

Beth Ann Fennelly

The Last Hummingbird of Summer

reveals itself in retrospect. Unlike the first,
whose March arrival bade you gasp, hands clasped,
like a child actor instructed to show joy, when the last
departs for points south, there's no telling,
and no tell. Well, so what? You know their cycle.
In August, they swarm the feeder, all swagger,
greedy tussle for sugar water. Suddenly,
September. Chill tickles your ankles. You reach
for long sleeves and you fret. They've left? Not yet.
Ear cocked for the symphony's shrinking strings.
Then comes a day without a ruby flash. Next day,
they're back. Next day, there's one. Then none.
Or maybe one? From porches, pumpkins grin.
Your last had left, and left you uninformed.

Kinda? Sorta? Can I say it?—like menstrual blood,
again, between your legs. Your last, perhaps,
or next-to-last, your no-longer-very-monthly
monthly. So unlike your first crimson, at twelve,
its "Yes-You-*Are*-There-God" annunciation.
Well, so what? You know the cycle. Your body's
eggy miracle, unneeded now for years.
And you hate waste. Why fill and dump
and fill again the undrunk sugar water?
Enough. Let's progress to whatever season's next.
But still, a farewell ritual wouldn't be amiss.
The last hummingbird of summer, zinging
from the feeder—to others, a smooth departure—
to you, alone, unmistakably, dipping its wing.

Molly Fisk

August

Smoke makes the air true, gruesome,
hangs thick between trees, curdles
noon light to a pink-orange-otherworldly

hue as if doom were visible and not just
a grinding in the solar plexus.
We can taste the pines, the ceanothus,

on our tongues, every incendiary twig
and sap-filled branch that has exploded
into ravenous flame. It's only our blaze

now in the river canyon boiling up but
a north wind is due that will lift fumes
from valley fires, spin them with those

beside the salt bay and bring new weather
to sear our throats. The whole state
is lightning-stunned, lit up and burning—

eucalyptus oils, laurel, black oak, coast
redwood, apricot and prune-plum, garlic
stems, cypress, artichokes charred

in their silver-green leaves, the heavy, staked
grapevines, harvest-laden. All ash
and memory. Mandarins, lemon groves.

Vievee Francis

Clarity (for Those Who Do Nothing but Hope)

Sorrow, O sorrow, moves like a loose flock
of blackbirds over the metal roofs, over the birches, and the miles.

     One wave after another, then another, then the sudden opening
where the feathered swirl, illumined by dusk, parts to reveal fire and flesh,
the true pink and weeping heart of everything.

Cruelty

April: the babble of Spring, like a belief in eternity:
the rain's innocent drop like sweet beads of sweat, the chirp,
buzz and drone, and all that sloshing in the birdbath, whispers like
the slide of one hand into another, tea stirred in the cups, songs sung and sung
and sung again as if any promise could be held in the short season of a hawthorn,
or could stop the silence that descends come fall's end. After the first snow
    reminds us
how alone we really are. And when the snows at last cease where will we be?
    And who?

CMarie Fuhrman

End Times

it's the last day of the earth
and I rise and feed my dogs, water
the Christmas cactus and spin off
the dying bloom. This, I am told, allows
for more blooms.

I'm not certain if the end is coming
by meteor or global war, or if the sparrow
will survive, but I put water in her bath, seed
in the feeder, and I don't kill the spider
which I wouldn't have before, either, before
I knew it was over.

What I will miss most is not knowing
the names of all the wildflowers, songs
of birds I've only met in books, languages
that will never be awoken.

It's the last day of the earth, and I've scrambled eggs,
as if dying a little hungry
would be punishment for so much consumption.

I have regrets.
Most come in the form of plastic toy hearts,
others are still smeared across my windshield.
It's the last day, and I have stolen
all the seed packets from the grocer's spinning stand

and I am casting them in the place
where we tried to grow a garden, the plot
below the house, the one we fenced off, then gave up on
back in the days we were certain
there would always be more.

Questioning the Sun

What shall I call you, he asked.
                    Sun, she replied.
And how shall I honor you, Sun?
                    Plant prayers on the Earth
What will those prayers reap?
                    Respect for the air life brings
And what shall I do when clouds come between us?
                    Believe I am still here
What shall I do when behind the mountains you fall?
                    Know that everything also rises
Shall I be as faithful to the moon?
                    It is as you are
Sun, may I wish on other stars?
                    If you wish with your deeds
I am afraid that you will burn up
                    I am afraid of burning you
When young gods are born, what fills their skies?
                    Earth
Sun, when we err, to whom do we beg forgiveness?
                    Your children
Sun, do you know disappointment?
                    I only know you
Sun, do you see our blue rising, our white glaciers disappearing?
                    Someday, too, shall I disappear
And then what, Sun
                    Then nothing
What will that be like?

Benjamin Garcia

Reasons for Abolishing Ice

with a first line by Bei Dao

because the ice age is over now	ice
because this isn't our first winter	ice
because the polar caps are melting	ice
because hands up if they say freeze	ice
because it's getting hard to breathe	ice
because it feels like walking on glass	ice
because crops are rotting in the field	ice
because it's clear it won't last forever	ice
because it looks like a diamond but isn't	ice
because you are here to take our people	ice
because I think we know enough of hate	ice
because we're gathering around the fire	ice
because snowflakes also cause whiteouts	ice
because you took the people out of police	ice
because I see you——I see you——I see you	ice
because black is considered more dangerous	ice
because they say the polar caps aren't melting	ice
because a person could slip through at any moment	ice

because you say we can't use our voice to launch an avalanche ice
because if you want papers then we'll crush you like booklice thumbed into paper

Michael Garrigan

Liturgy of Carp Becoming a God

Find an island thick with knotweed
    and two white egrets stalking shallows,
wade downstream along the bank pausing every few feet
    to let the river show you how to be,
to make sure that the rocks and ledges you see
    are what they are and not what you want them to be.
Climb over the trunk of a lightning-struck river birch,
    look into water, and you are still, let your eyes adjust,
find a school of seven large carp brushing their scales against sunken
    branches. Breathe until you begin to blend, slowly kneel
until knees hit soft sediment that's soaked for most of the year
    but it's August and the river is thirsty,
and these carp, they are shuffling like stalks of corn in mourning wind
    and everything moves as if we're caught in a hidden riverland hymn.
And you are still. Follow their rhythms until you notice
    they are taking turns swimming into the deep
channel to suck down little damselfly nymphs, letting water usher them
    into the shallow end of the pool where they feel it slow and scoot
quick up under the deadfall waiting their turn and your fingers
    are in the water reaching for their tails hoping to touch one
since you can't seem to land one with your fly rod
    and now your palm is wet and you brush off the memory
of a wafer turned into body amen and a long walk back to your pew
    as the next carp takes its turn you slide
your whole arm in and let it become water and you are still
    and haven't breathed in a few seconds
and you think you finally found the right words to build a prayer
    that will be heard and when you exhale they notice you,
because that's what Gods do, notice,
    and they dart off into the deep current and your
palms are left open and once sediment settles
    you consider sliding your whole body into water
to become a river-prayer-flag forever caught in current.

Ross Gay

A Small Needful Fact

Is that Eric Garner worked

for some time in the Parks and Rec.
Horticultural Department, which means,

perhaps, that with his very large hands,
perhaps, in all likelihood,

he put gently into the earth
some plants which, most likely,
some of them, in all likelihood,
continue to grow, continue

to do what such plants do, like house

and feed small and necessary creatures,
like being pleasant to touch and smell,
like converting sunlight

into food, like making it easier
for us to breathe.

Becoming a Horse

It was dragging my hands along its belly,
loosing the bit and wiping the spit
from its mouth that made me
a snatch of grass in the thing's maw,
a fly tasting its ear. It was
touching my nose to his that made me know
the clover's bloom, my wet eye to his that
made me know the long field's secrets.
But it was putting my heart to the horse's that made me know
the sorrow of horses. Made me
forsake my thumbs for the sheen of unshod hooves.
And in this way drop my torches.
And in this way drop my knives.
Feel the small song in my chest
swell and my coat glisten and twitch.
And my face grow long.
And these words cast off, at last,
for the slow honest tongue of horses.

Melissa Ginsburg

So attached you are to living in the world

Cut off access to the feeding stream and the water will come instead from
    below. Will rise
and form puddles on the hill, even in dry weather.

The pattern of woven and knitted grasses, the plethora of knots worked
    by wind—like you,
it undoes

everything it does. Reckless skies, falling trees, horizon floating like
    algae.
You try to see yourself from the outside, where the weather

is spinning. You identify with the largest predator
because she never lets you near. Ruthless,

unabating in her shyness. Through this unseasonal flowering
the heron keeps spearing tadpoles. You can see her but you can't

get as close as you'd like. You lose track of your mind in the satellite
    photo. Are you
the solitary wood duck, its markings sleeker without the flock? Are you

the heron's wet legs, are you the straight-line wind?
Are you your own mistake, your own darling? Again and again you ocean
    the marsh,

lock the hurricane in the bathtub.
You walk straight into the spider's web and close its door behind you.

Sarah Giragosian

Newtok, Alaska

home of the Yup'ik, the earth's first climate refugees

There's not much time left,
            the elders tell us.
                The river slurps at the edges
of our village, and we bury our hungers in work.
       We raise homes on stilts to ballast
           ourselves atop the ancient permafrost,
              but it melts faster than we can build.
Sinking, we sing our children to sleep
               in careening bedrooms, string up and dry
      strips of pike while the land pitches below our feet,
          mush our dog teams across a crackling Jacob's ladder
            of ice. The borders of our world are shrinking:
our kids go jigging for burbot and herring
              from their front doors; we've seen them toeing
the drop-off point like seal pups testing their power
              and playing caribou eye in corners
where tundra's thin as teeth
         ground down to gums
         and sour dock sprouts from slush.

There's not much time left,
           and outsiders tell us to start over in Anchorage,
             city of disappearances, before we are swallowed up
by sea. We prepare to move to higher ground:
     we apply for funds, pray the government will help.
           Exile is expensive and the elders are slipping away.
            They say their dreams are invaded by ice-
music, sounds of cracking and whomping so loud,
   they wake with chipped teeth
         and the taste of sea brine in their mouths.

Jody Gladding

[grass widow / grass stained]

why

was I

always

in love

with   the

grass

widow

sharp-tongued

blades

cut

witch

grass

stained

my hands

was I

not

her

kind

Rigoberto González

from Apocalipsixtlán

[5. SIGNS OF THE END OF THE WORLD]

The right path. The phrase echoes in our heads
   as we travel west, away from the crack in the earth.
There is no way around it. Some say it connects
   Tierra del Fuego to the North Pole and cuts deep
down to the core—a wound that lets the heat escape
   each minute of the day. When all of the Américas
became a desert, dividing coast from coast, those
   caught in the middle either sunk into the crevice
or sunk into despair. *The right path.* That's what
   Those Who Came Before tried to sell us before hell

rose from the bowels of the planet to burn the air
   in every lung. When the animals began to flee
and the birds headed east, we should have guessed
   the doom had come upon us then. But the right path
was not to panic but to *study* these changes, *discuss*
   policy, hold town meetings—negotiate. Catastrophe
was just another balloon to deflate. By the time
   the ground beneath our feet began to shake, it
was already too late to save our cities, which had
   turned to liquid we couldn't drink. Next came thirst.

What comedy to witness humans think they're
   in control of anything. The new collectives with
the old were just as tired and useless as the past.
   Their lifetime of mistake and misdirection was what
had killed us. Why repeat the leadership? Why
   allow the yesterday to roll its ancient wheels
into the present? Oh preachers of pretense, we
   silenced you. Oh teachers of nonsense, we erased
you. The future is ours, you all said, and the future
   arrived, bleak and black, but with much less room

to move around. A future without windows or doors,
    and one ugly hole in the ground that offers no escape.
What future is this? we asked. And Those Who Came
    Before simply shrugged their shoulders and shook
their heads. When the gas discharged from the opening
    we smelled the answer—sour odor of crimes against
the land and the centuries of death that had been buried
    there. Out flew centuries of damage and buried bodies
to hover above us like magpies shrieking: *The crack*
    in the earth, it is us. The crack in the earth, it is ours.

[12. A SECOND CRACK IN THE EARTH]

The pond of bones begins to rattle. Even Mother's
    throne collapses, her body disassembles. The ground
turns to quicksand as it trembles and swallows
    every socket, every thorn, every pebble. In a single
gulp the bed beneath the Smaller Ones swirls down
    a funnel. The earth has groaned like this before.
We know what to expect though it doesn't help
    us guess which plate will lift its crust and which
will crumble. The dust is blinding. It separates us
    as we scramble. Unknowingly, some of us run

right into the opening and plummet. We hear
    no screams. We hear no cough though we see us
spitting ink—the gas unleashed has cooked our
    lungs. Slowly the collective gathers in the shadow
of the clouds. We must guide our shattered spirits
    to a shelter before the mists release their acid.
In our ears the ringing doesn't stop. It will take
    a week and some of us will get the sickness—that
rabid urge to kill and tear apart what's whole.
    We fear no second crack. We fear another purge.

We wrap our arms around our bodies, swaying back
    and forth—we're motherless cradles, candle stubs
whose flames have melted down to callus. We are
    silent but for the piercing shrill inside our heads.
Cocooned in misery, we might have missed this
    spark of light entirely, but there it is, lifting heavy

chins from chests: a firefly—an actual firefly,
   beautiful bug from our fantasy game, a reality
here among the detritus of the world, rising from
   its dregs, a flicker, a flash, a wink of vital breath.

We try to catch the little star but it eludes our grasp.
   We let it be, it comes to rest upon a knee. Dare we
ask if this means the planet now spins in opposite
   direction? Does it begin to mend its ruptures, unclog
its river paths? The firefly fades but its ghost remains.
   No more dreams, no more questions. Sleep, tiny hope,
we do not know what threats or sorrows we'll
   encounter next. Tomorrow is a story for those who
make it through the present chronicle—uncertainty,
   scarcity—we the ephemeral have inherited this earth.

Andrew Gottlieb

The Inner Wild

Far away, I think of Wu Mountain Light,
blossoms ablaze and a clear warm river.
— LI PO, TRANSLATED BY DAVID HINTON

Remembering alder along the river,
the shiver of aspen. Hiking the gravel
in the inch of water on the inside curve
of the river's whims. You were about to cast
and the moose stepped free from the tangle
of the far shoulder's willow.
                                          Later, the hawk
heading for the red cliffs, the whitetails
flushed as you crunch through the dry meadow.
The desire to follow. To find belonging
among the wet pebbles shifting in our palm,
the red spots on a brown trout's side.
To bed down in wild grass, to sleep with a river.
To try to name the question that memory
always is,
                    black eye flashing in the mirror
that we are: untethered, flowing, gone.

Robin Gow

Kill Your Local Lanternfly

The way you might open a soda tab
or run your fingers across an itchy postage of skin.

How a window cracks from a hurtled rock.
Exactly like a rift the moon's dancing skirt.

Not to be concerned with after. Thumb licked
and pressed to the flame's forehead.

Who knows where the souls of insects
fit themselves. How or why they linger.

Haunting the parking lots of our fathers.
Reborn, the lanternfly will be quelled just as before.

With the hinge of a knee. Months of formation
flattened and scattered. Scab disintegrating

back into skin. I want a scar in the shape
of my species. Where will our skeletons sleep

without the threat of extermination?
A graveyard for lanternflies where each headstone

is nothing but a thumb. An open palm to land on.
Soft whir of the next jump. Leaves nodding
$\qquad\qquad\qquad\qquad\qquad$ as they watch.

Lanternflies Dream of Being Butterflies

To be captured not
like contagion
but feather or cottonwood.
Beloved and specimen.
Children in their schoolyards
releasing us and recounting our
life cycles like prayers: egg,
caterpillar, chrysalis,
and butterfly. To sleep through
change instead of morphing.
Each day a step closer
to drinking the souls of trees.
All I want is the ease
of being the right kind of
beautiful. To amble as a
body should—
unfettered and ungendered.
Ready for another migration.
Always following the warm chest of
the sun. How does it feel
to be worshipped?
Adoration, another kind
of exoskeleton. Eating sugar
from a daffodil's eager face.
Yellow sweetness. Satisfaction
spun through every limb.
Wind making postage stamps
of my wings. Oh! How I would
find mirrors to marvel
at my own patterns. How I would
pulse my new wet wings
like watercolors.

Maggie Graber

in which i notice the birds again

today the angels are happy. the heart is a garden
buzzing in early september after a sun-soaked summer
& i'm a tree in a forest. someone knocks on me like a door
that won't open. i'm hard in the places i need to be
& soft everywhere else. buddhism teaches
the container is already broken, the heart
a sponge wrung dry. i believe it & a bird
testifies, then another, then another until even
the grasshopper's flappity wing is the net i've cast.
if an astronaut cries in orbit the tears stay in their eyes
& they can't see. i watch *sabrina the teenage witch*
with my hulu-spotify subscription & say
magic. the other week i found part of an animal
jawbone with a couple teeth near my house.
sometimes i feel like a record that always skips
in the same place: capricorn in the sun, scorpio
in the moon, like a hallway in an enchanted castle.
when everything's alive, what happens to the dead?
once my heart slid safe into home. the anthill
wasn't destroyed. my time on earth summarized
as one in which i've noticed the birds again,
feet paddling under water, closed eyes drawn like clamshells.
i straighten my back, give some air to the cavernous chakra
in my chest, remember birmingham, alabama,
star wars night at the barons game, fireworks & droids, bee
on a wood spoon, view from my friend's bungalow overlooking the city
through a clearing in some branches, plants winding up the staircase
toward a rainbow flag. here is the fire, the forest
& the garden. here are the birds again. i know
some of their names. & my friends, the plants—
all they do is stand in the backyard & drink the light.
they turn the light into sugar.
of course they do.

Dana J. Graef

On the Creek

December 5, 2020, and cherry blossoms are blooming beside the holly. The berries are there, ripening and red, the leaves thick and thorny in their winter sturdiness. On one side of the driveway, those berries. On the other, those blossoms, pink, light, and fragile in the cold. The light is thin and reflecting off the water in pale blue. Soon the sun will set and around the neighborhood, masked, one at a time and in pairs, people are walking. Past the blooming cherries, past the berries, and around the corner, leaves: red and orange, maple leaves, leaves of fall. The sun on everything. The seasons swirling. The days darkening. The air cold. How long have I spent, walking toward docks on this quiet creek? How many times have I seen the jellyfish pulsing, and the herons, and the sunlight glinting, and the water that rises and falls with the moon and the rain and the daily tides? This place—it turns toward water. It has marsh grasses and muddiness—and I am in the midst of it. But then the water flows, out from this creek to the bay, out from this bay to the ocean, the open, warming ocean, where a month ago the waves were pulling horseshoe crabs, lifeless, in and out of the foam. Others had landed on the beach. The sun illuminated each one like softened amber sitting on the sand. I think I should have more to say. Something that brings it all together: the jellyfish, the herons, the horseshoe crabs; the tides, the moon; the blossoms, the waves. My thoughts are fleeting. But I know that if I sit on the dock on this tidal creek, for a moment I can stretch my mind and flow with the water. Soon, I am back in the ocean. And amidst the swirling brokenness of it all, there is salt air, and death that looks like amber—and then the sunlight shatters on the creek.

Miriam Bird Greenberg

• [Whole towns like • horses turnt loose]

Paradise, California

Whole towns like • horses turnt loose in the bardo of •
« wild » fire's roiling, locust-clouded « our » stampede—as if
ignoring a war two counties over meant it couldn't come
closer—of plague-black | ened forests consumed by a burnt
• wind: « and untamable » lithe and lumbering creature cities-
sized, mitosis-prone, come to lick clean the tinder « tender
ly » face of village midstampede. Caressing • lost wedding
pictures, kitchen tables, • dogs lured in « runaway » terror in
to the inferno. It leaps roads in its roving. Whole towns re
made over • and faraway in « night » parking lots where « wander »
in daze • once-middle-class refugees the fire's made. There, atop
an RV, a parrot's perched, and for its human from whom
it's learned, its gift: *Fuck you*, it says. Its every instinct • breach
ed, and blackened « trust- » in human-made ruin. *Hello?*

• [In Paradise the fire ate]

Paradise, California

In Paradise the fire ate, *dulce et decorum est,* more than eighty
(so far known), average age of seventy-nine. In • Ab
original cultures, communities avoid saying even « certain »
even syllables occurring in names of the recent
ly deceased. "That old lady" they'd say instead, giving re
spect to s | kin of sea | turtle, saltwater, crane. Their names
unknowns—*untils*—until forensics comes to Paradise
's dead to make their claim. Newborns cradled in their mothers'
arms • in nurses' personal cars, or « rode » elders drinking oxygen
from • mask. Imagine « its » • in « yourself » enclosed vehicle of panic
's un | natural spreading darkness • that swept « of flame » roads
ides faster than you drove. In gridlock gasped a student,
pointing at the moon—ripened full in the Feather River's night
bound sky. *No,* their teacher (driving) said while « fell, » a midday
rain of soot • that's the sun, child, *ardent for some desperate glory.*

Lilace Mellin Guignard

Fracked Pastoral

Tioga County, Pennsylvania, 2010

Like my daughter's sash undone, the road
waves this and that way, then stops behind gas
trucks. I can't see beyond the signs "residual
waste." Some dumpers, some round tanks, all machines
stacked like a deck against us getting home
any time soon. The rest of the family

won't worry. This happens often. Family
dinners are hard to pull off, rare as backroads
unclogged or unpocked. A wire-perched hawk homes
in on some small heart, field-hid. So much gas—
everything runs on something. We're all machines
in this garden, this countryside of residual

family farms, leftover know-how, skills a residual
effect of past necessity. Cows are family.
New dairy barns dot the hills. Inside, machines
take the place of hands. Our journey down this road
started long ago. My daughter starts to cry. We need gas
but are only inching hill by hill home.

"Have a lollipop. We'll eat when we get home."
I hand the treat into the back seat, my residual
stash from Halloween hidden in my purse with gas
money. It's May and that's the last one. Family
bills weigh down more than my purse. The road
will not end, will not speed up. "Goddamn machines!

Fucking trucks!" *Don't cuss.* Pointing at the machines
my girl says, "fucking trucks." If we were home
I'd put us both in time-out, but here just laugh. The road
pitches down again and we speed up, residual
momentum carrying us uphill a little farther to family,
passing by gas pad after drill rig after brine pond after gas

pad—back to a house where dinner cooked by natural gas
is long cold. I don't know how to break this cycle. Machines
have nothing over humans' inability to stop on our own. Family
is what slows me, grounds me, makes me pull over at home.
I can only pray there is some unwasted wisdom, residual
in human bones, some way to steer us down another road.

Wee wee wee want gas all the way home,
but machines don't play games, don't have families,
and I can't tell if hope is a road or merely an instinct, residual.

Kelsea Habecker

Self-Portrait with Salmon

The beach is netted with debris:
      fish-skeleton etchings, coolers leak

ice, men snore face-down
      in the sand, exhausted by the long

daylit night of waiting for salmon.
      Sad spectacle, the huddle of tents

along ryegrass dunes, plastic sleds stacked
      with firewood wet after the morning rain,

the scattered scales glinting
      along a grime-scalloped shore.

Waist-deep in chest waders and elbow
      to elbow, we stand amassed in the mouth

of the river emptying into ocean,
      our aluminum hoop nets catching nothing

but tide. A mile out the commercial boats
      snag everything. You could call it faith

that keeps us standing here, cold-toed
      and weary of water, or the need to combat

a living thing, feel the strain against net
      that quickens pulse and brain.

Beyond us seals bark a rebuke we know
      by name. We ignore it, so great

the need to hold down a writhing
      silvered muscle, rip out the gills

and blade the body to expose the pink meat.
      How like lungs it looks. How like fish we feel

swimming toward death. We work quickly to gut,
      finger the heart still lurching.

Aaron Hand

Glimpses of Wilderness

It will happen in the parking lot. The one where concrete gave way to the convocation of dandelions and the spike of thistle waits in the flower of the sun to claw the softness of a bare foot. Where the shag spurge rugs over what's left of white figures in wheelchairs and foxtails strongarm the golden lines into dust. The one with the old tire that lost its Faultline treads to the heavy hand of the road and now sits collecting wrigglers into its rainfull belly as the prostrating knotweed sips the slosh of overflow. A crash of quack grass kisses the corners of a brown corduroy couch that looks like a ghost of your grandmother's couch but this one slouches toward Bethlehem Day Care with its boarded-up windows and fading mural of a giraffe that once held a smile as it sticks its long neck out of the top of Noah's Ark. The missing leg gnawed away by mice that made a home of its hollow body: cotton collecting in one corner and droppings in another. There, in this parking lot, among the anthills, crabgrass, chickweed, and clovers. Among the rusty nails, coke cans, and tumbleweed. Among the creeping charlie and the galaxy of glass. There, with the rattle of gravel under each of your tender footsteps, you will see your first naked body in the sprawl of wind torn pages of a porno mag dated from before you were born. Holding a glance slightly longer than your mother would approve of, you study how the wilderness of hair blooms down a body: first, cascading across the chest, and once over the edge, it spreads through the symmetrical hills of the abdomen. From there it fades bare like swidden farmland, until the boulder of thigh welcomes the new growth and you see that the grove doesn't stop until it reaches the last bit of knuckle on the big toe. And there, you will see the juniper of hair hanging over the edge, bracing for the coming wind.

Eman Hassan

To the Beach with My Nephew

Kuwait, 2004

It's in the way we hold a sandwich
in each hand: I relish the drive, recall light-blue
skies of my youth, turn my back on soot-heavy black

        now spewing from the Ahmadi Oil Refinery we ride by:
  uncapped flares smoking like dirty dinars lighting the desert on fire

for more. This refinery resembles New York City at night to those who know

and dream of being somewhere else, maybe over there
though we savor the cheap falafel wraps over here.

Once we reach the shore, I tell Little Ant how clean the deep used to be.

Now barnacles form
    on Styrofoam,
           wind hurls the white-tipped whorls forward
like a heartbeat,
like a refinery
that never sleeps.

I want to say *Enough, oh Sea,* like in that b&w Kuwaiti movie, but waves
  keep coming.

Two hermit crabs locked in battle:
it's in the way their claws grip together.

My nephew means well, jumps to interfere,
tries to save the smaller from becoming the larger one's meal

        but the waves keep coming and we are in Manhattan
          looking out a window over the Hudson.

Gisela Heffes

An Epistemology of Floriculture

I would say it is the place where sorrow lies.
— JUAN RULFO, "LUVINA"

I received roses today.
Roses from the savanna of Bogotá
I don't like roses.
Much less from Colombia.

The flowers in Colombia are sprayed with pesticides.
The women who work in the floriculture industry are exposed to the
    pesticides.
The women who work in the floriculture industry cannot procreate.
Their uteruses cannot harbor another life (only their own, maybe).
The life of the flower suppresses, eliminates, erases the human life that is
    yet unborn, unable to develop.

The flowers of the savanna gleam in google images.
Inside, the women smile, happy.
Outside, the hats protect their faces from the sun.
The flowers are colorful and brilliant.
        Bouquets for Mother's Day.
        Roses for Valentine's Day.
        Flowers to celebrate graduations, a new job, the arrival of a newborn.

The abdomen smooth and flat.
A belly without a bellybutton.
Premature births.
Birth defects.
Congenital malformations.

Who uses flowers from the savanna of Bogotá?
Who celebrates life with flowers that cut it off?
Who imports flowers regardless?
Regardless of what?
Regardless of so much.

Don't buy me flowers.
Don't send me roses.
Much less from the savanna.
From Bogotá.
From Colombia.

— Translated by Adele Lonas

Kathleen Hellen

big weary

Mosquitoes in their gigantism gather in the thunder.
In clay—a human wailing.
      Some say snakes
slither like the river
to beginnings. Some say
there were nations, tribes,
detailed in the carcasses of fish.
No more cattails, plover.
      With eyes of ancient trilobites
I see the signals: the crab smokestacked, the thorny plant
escaping in the mouths of vipers

downriver
where trees grow stilts. I witness: wheat chest-high
waiting on the combine, swamped in dirty water.
Rice can't head to higher ground from silos.
Witness: pigs
snorkeling, a raft of squawking chickens.
Cows sucked under.

In pyramids of tires
these houses plywood shuttered
fool themselves—thunder
crows hammers. The levee quits
in narrows. Mothers swim
away. They go to live with aunties gilled
for dissolutions.

I've never known a river that was straighter
than it should be, mattressed by refineries, the thin-
lipped mouth of it sipping runoff from
the corn farms jumping states. All is sniff-me shrimp,
the empty suitcases of oysters
carpeting the trawlers.
Nothing easy

in the confluence of
what we know and what we've only
guessed
      carried downstream and hell roaring
like wild hogs at Angola.
I've never known a river that was shortened,

blasted, grassed against high water,
against the blessed open spaces.
Some who live
invent the blues
croaking from the back-of-throat
like alligators.

W. J. Herbert

The End of Immortality

Human activity has made growing new stems much tougher for
[the ten-thousand-year-old Pando grove].
— FAYE FLAM, WASHINGTON POST, APRIL 9, 2023

So many rescued were turned into trees.
     Daphne into a laurel, Myrrha nursing
          her baby on a sweet band of cambium

& even though I didn't see aspens
     branching above me or hear the wind
          ripple through their leaves' ragged teeth,

as I breathed they murmured inside me,
     greening my lungs with their whispers
          & gossip. Is it so hard to believe

     that I wanted to be what they made of me?—

Though fewer seedlings born of roots
     the grove set to bind itself together,
          fewer clones of the spawning tree

survive, still I wanted to wear this bark,
     these branches coated with antler's velvet
          & lichens' mustardy dust;

eyes, lips, tongue gone to mosses, seep
     of springs at my feet, roots fanning out
          to the far edge of memory.

Claudia D. Hernández

The River Never Happened to Us (ii.)

We walked more than a thousand miles to get to the other side of
the Rio Bravo, guided by the Coyote's howl. We didn't bathe in the

river.

Instead, we floated like thin paper boats, tanned by the sun.
I don't remember caressing the surface of any pumice

rock.

I stuck my fingers between cottonwood crevices, their
trunks rooted on opposite sides of the river. We were

bound

to eat desert wind; I was ten. When we reached the other
side, we hid behind bushes; quietly, we sank slowly in the

mud.

When the Coyotes signaled, we walked, no, we ran and our knees
shed broken pieces of mud. No one drowned in the river; no one had

to be

resuscitated from the mud. Yet we continued to trickle
shards of mud, as if the river had never happened to us.

Tiffany Margaret Higgins

Chewing the Sun

Belém do Pará, Amazônia, Brazil

All night smoke drifts
through the windows

bits of leaves and trees

lives of others
arrive on the air

lizards and *tatus*
(armadillos)
capivaras

the slow sloths
hand over hand
never flee
fast enough

smoke lines the throat
a film moves
across my eyes

around no one
seems to heed

Far in the interior, a parrot nest
in the just-felled forest

a green ghost comes crying
orphaned through the *galhos*

someone sets the grand
Brazil nut trees alight
some hand-fires the palms

we sleep in the ashes

men of meat
send soy to far-off kingdoms
to be fed to meat

animal orders
the breathing green
replaced
by pale steers
chewing equatorial sun

with each flank,
we are warming
to our subject

the death
of all we loved

of death
we all loved

it comes in slow
breath by breath
not so you'd notice

there was forest
they said there was
so much of it

Sean Hill

The White-Headed Woodpecker

Quiet. Given to prying more than pecking, an odd member
of the family, lives only in the high pine forests of western

mountains like the Cascades, where I spent an afternoon
almost a decade ago in Roslyn, Washington, looking for what

I could find of Black people who'd migrated from the South
almost a century and a quarter prior. The white-headed

woodpecker doesn't migrate and so is found in its
home range year-round when it can be found. Roslyn,

founded as a coal mining town, drew miners from all over
Europe—as far away as Croatia—across the ocean, with

opportunities. With their hammering and drilling to extract
a living, woodpeckers could be considered arboreal miners.

A habitat, a home range, is where one can feed and house
oneself—meet the requirements of life—and propagate.

In 1888, those miners from many lands all in Roslyn came
together to go on strike against the mine management.

And so, from southern states, a few hundred Black miners
were recruited with the promise of opportunities in Roslyn,

many with their families in tow, to break the strike. They
faced resentment and armed resistance, left in the dark

until their arrival, unwitting scabs—that healing that happens
after lacerations or abrasions. Things settled down as they do

sometimes, and eventually Blacks and whites entered a union
as equals. Black save for a white face and crown and a sliver

of white on its wings that flares to a crescent when they
spread for flight, the white-headed woodpecker is a study

in stark contrasts. Males have a patch of red feathers
on the back of their crowns, and I can't help but see blood.

Rick Hilles

Tell Me

Just an hour away from
the latest train derailment

where toxins still seep
into Ohio groundwater

and land where I grew up
there can still be birdsong

a brown river rippling
with current, mica flecks

of light like flint. And I
hear honking and see one

full-grown male mallard
attempting to mount

a female clearly mated
to another, the one

ramming his bill into
the assailant while two

others paddle away
I want to say   *in shame.*

By now all three males
hide in the high reeds

at the water's edge
pecking each other

like *The Three Stooges*
the one TV show

mom wouldn't let us watch—
too violent and cruel.

And is that where it all
begins? The first question

that says not everything
is for me? Something

definitely is not right
in the air today an almost

chemical burn that no
amount of winter softens

from what I take in each time
I breathe. And yet the trees

take it in too exhaling from it
more and more of what we need.

Yet the air leaves a strange aftertaste
like I've been tonguing batteries

to make sure they're still good.
Is this all then just my way of

putting the world to my mouth?
And finding what's still good in it.

Which may be why I need you
to tell me, am I still part of what

is good and true among what lives?

Caroline Hockenbury

Machete

When people eat chocolate, they are eating my flesh.
— DRISSA, NOW FREE

My memory reaches first for the bowl, big
and plastic and rimmed by ghosts, gaping

like an open mouth from where it sits,
an orange invitation on the porch,

taking up space *(Take what you wish!)*
and anticipating the hands—most tiny,

some bigger, many sticky
or gloved—that will want

to gobble up the air between
costumed bodies and the chocolate,

the chocolate wrapped in silver
foil, portioned like little gifts, heaped

on top of itself into a happy landmass
of minibars, some falling down the sides

like clods of dark earth kicked
from a peak or shifting stones stolen

by gravity: the same pull that resists
lift in a child's wrist when, in the Ivory Coast,

he steadies his breathing and readies
the machete, glinting silver as a blade

of light pierces the forest's outer wall
and moves toward him, a boy

who has grown to anticipate the terrible
crack that cries out in the forest

every time a cocoa pod severs
into husk and flesh, revealing

the beans—outlined in wet and pressed
along the shell's strong jaw—like ivory teeth

that grimace against his fingers
as he wrestles out the connections between

the precious bits, the white treasure
that must sit and dry and wait

while he unfurls a blanket of chemicals
over his crops, his skin, his only protection

maybe the drooping lips of a bucket hat
touching his ears just at the tips

while he makes a moon of his body, his back
bending toward sacks, tan and matching

his weight: a number unaccounted for
like the years he's now spent

not sitting in a schoolhouse,
not phoning home to his family,

not boarding a bus back
to Burkina Faso, the home he stole

away from in order to take in roughly
85 cents a day by wielding a weapon

in thick wilderness somewhere. Out there,
pillowcases moonlight as candy sacks,

unrelenting pendulums that swing
and thwack kids' knees while they orbit

the neighborhood on Halloween night.
Some find their way to a bus stop

elsewhere. Some are as young as ten.
Some carry chainsaws among the leaves.

Cynthia Marie Hoffman

Ecotherapy

Today, on the prairie boardwalk, there's a death
stench it's impossible to get away from. Perhaps
an animal floats in the water, secretly bloating
beneath the lid of this human-laid casket.
Only the darkness in the pond knows. I kneel,
scoop a palmful of duck weed from the surface
and with it, delicate roots come trailing
like filaments that transmit signals from the brain.
I receive my own dark signals. Like the idea
this smell of rot is the boardwalk itself,
and today is the day I'll fall through. The therapist
says when I'm feeling this way to go on a walk
but doesn't say whether to come back.
Here are some berries I've never seen before,
maybe poisonous. Here comes a dragonfly
whose black wings are the windows
of the church of darkness clamping shut.
How long would it take someone to find me
drowned in the dark mind of the pond?
Once, a friend scooped a dead rabbit from her yard,
walked the trail two miles with it
in a shoebox in her arms, and dug a hole

with her trowel beneath the picturesque oak.

No one dared say a thing while she dug

and buried. And now I follow this trail,

unsure what my purpose is. Around the bend,

a bumblebee darts out of the way

just in time to avoid a collision

with my forehead. For a moment, we

see eye to eye. Neither of us wants to die.

Marybeth Holleman

she *zompopas*

*A society grows great when old people plant trees whose shade
they will never sit under.*
— GREEK PROVERB

                            17 years ago,
when her son was 12 and she not yet 45, she
returned home determined that when he fledged
she'd move to the jungle and study them,
this line of ants each carrying a big green sail.
leaf-cutters are everywhere here, their trails joining
and crossing hers, tunneling under fallen branches,
teetering along spines of thick roots, wearing down
leaf duff with the hundreds or thousands moving
in both directions, one way all carrying
the other way all not, but all heading toward.
                         they are everywhere,
they carry up to 50 times their body weight,
consume 15 percent of the leafdense jungle, live
in symbiotic harmony, farming fungus who eats
the leaves and gives them food. they are seen as pests
to farmers who destroy them by killing their queen.
                         they are all
female, every single green-sailed one, the queen
and her legions of workers, all following the scent trail
of scouts to the plants they have chosen. like the Votos,
or the Diquis, those now-exterminated small tribes
led by chieftainesses, the Costa Rican *indigenes*,
who left behind only *bolas di pietra*, petrospheres
like underground mounds of anthills,
                         they are female-
led, males only appearing when the colony
must split, a new queen must be bred. then,
skies fill with flying males who live long enough
to provide the next generation. who are all female,

every small moving sail, their trails now along pink
fallen petals and over crushed mango and through
rotting log, so many so everywhere that she works hard
not to step on them, not to squander a single moment
of their life, of hers, not to harm a single ant

                              who works hard,
carries weight, keeps moving, her life's
work always toward the benefit of the whole.

Erin Coughlin Hollowell

Wrack Line

you place your feet   on the boundary

   moon creates   by pulling

      earth creates   by tipping

   dark line scribed   across cobbles

across shadow sand   across drifts of pebbles

what makes language   from decay

   of sea grown frill   small lives missing float

     you move along, between   sandstone bluffs

   wash of waves, there are   centuries exposed

tooth of mammoth   spinal column of otter

   blue plastic toy   tumbled faceless

     water hisses   clicks shatters stones

     thunders roll-gallops   brushes brushes

   your feet know   your ears know

nests of branch strewn   three stripped feathers

emptied crablings   wind knocks stone

   gathering river   tang, mudflat silt

     wrack riddled   boundary shifting

Choreographic

The sea is infinitely patient, each wave
saying to the stones of shore *whist whist whist*.

Or are they saying *wish*? As in don't you wish

your world was one continuous muscle of movement,
an engine of flux? The waves place a thumb
on each stone and rub, taking away a bit here,

a fragment there. They think the stone is subdued.

Anyone who stands beneath the bluffs knows
differently. Stones ride the waves in a concert
of clicking and chattering. That rumble you

think is the wave's voice, it's really the stones

using the ocean to speak, like a flute
uses breath to form its silver swinging.

Marie Howe

Postscript

What we did to the earth, we did to our daughters
one after the other.

What we did to the trees, we did to our elders
stacked in their wheelchairs by the lunchroom door.

What we did to our daughters, we did to our sons
calling out for their mothers.

What we did to the trees, what we did to the earth,
we did to our sons, to our daughters.

What we did to the cow, to the pig, to the lamb,
we did to the earth, butchered and milked it.

Few of us knew what the birdcalls meant
or what the fires were saying.

We took of earth and took and took, and the earth
seemed not to mind

Until one of our daughters shouted: *it was right
in front of you, right in front of your eyes*

and you didn't see.
The air turned red.   The ocean grew teeth.

Richard Jackson

An Ending of Sorts

Eternity is in love with the productions of time.
— WILLIAM BLAKE

When you face the sun as it begins to slide down
the other side of the ridge, all that fills the eye is
light,
    and when you turn away the dark spots are
like the day stars just starting to smudge the sky.

What we don't see is a whole forest of desires.

A patchwork of deer trails leading to, to where?

Beyond, cylinders of hay line the field.
                            I want to
believe there is no end to this trail.
                        Here, surface
roots write indecipherable messages in Kanji.

Branches write and erase their own shadows
with the wind.
           As a boy I'd run a path like this
that fell off sixty feet on either side.
                      I should
have died back then.
              One of us did.
              The past,
like these words, rises up from the mind's tunnels
as unexpectedly as voles.
                There is always a hawk
or owl whose shadow rakes the ground for them.

Just here, the path is marked with the tracks
of so many animals, as if, unlike us, they had
learned to live together.
            Everything that lives is holy,
Blake wrote.

This evening, Venus, just now,
rises over Jupiter and I would like to believe
it is a sign that means *love over power.*
                         The redbuds
have started to reveal their own secrets,
                              the gingko is
waiting for the right time.
                    This trail is never the same
trail.
         Branch fall, shifting glacier age boulders,
the field mouse nervous across my path, the opossum
fear frozen.
         Here, nothing is ever in the wrong place
even when it is in the wrong place.
                              I would like to
believe that the end would be always just beginning.

I would like, in the end, to be these woods.

We all live in the borrowed light of the moon.

Jessica Jacobs

And the Ground Opens Its Mouth to Speak

*And God said to Cain, "Cursed are you from the ground that
opened its mouth to take your brother's blood from your hand."*
— GENESIS 4:10–11

Dear wandering dust, dear vagrant clay,
dear humans made of me,

how quickly you've forgotten.
I am not just a backdrop
for your horrors—

read your holy book: Stars and trees
join in battle, hills mourn, valleys
and waves shudder and writhe

at the approach of God. And how
many of your slaughtered
have I choked down?

Your clearcuts evict owls,
salamanders, wolves so you can build
your houses in hills now primed

for fire. I am trying
to warn you. For every season,
I send wrong weather, drain

reefs of their color, let whole species
go extinct. Yet you go on.
Enough. Too much.

Protagonist, delinquent. Who are you
in this story:

Seeing something he wanted
across the road, a boy dropped
his mother's hand

and ran into the snarl
of traffic. She screamed his name,
rooted there, unable to look away.

At the clamor and rush, at a mirror hissing
so close past his ear it raised
the small hairs inside it,

he ran back to her. Weeping,
she slapped him, hard; weeping,
he pressed the heat of his cheek

to her chest. That slap? Pain now
to stave off worse later. A mark
to carry with him and remember.

I am so tired of being afraid
for you.

Elizabeth Jacobson

There Are as Many Songs in the World
as Branches of Coral

I walk a long way
sinking in soft sand.

My feet, two creatures
of burden.

Low-lying clouds
mirror stormy ocean waves

and wild eddies.
The wrack line

littered with elkhorn
with coral sponges—

each one a finger
from a different hand.

Disappeared
are the reefs

they arose from.
As a child

I combed black rocks of a jetty
prying starfish from pools

sucked salt
off their legs,

curious podia searching
my tongue.

I craved also
the taste of ash

ate cigarette butts
from the beach—

put anything in my mouth
to know it.

•

I was nine
when I first saw the photographs—

bodies overflowing
from wheelbarrows.

Corpses pitched
in heaps like firewood

at the sides of barracks.
Didn't recognize what they were.

Then I noticed the bird,
a raven,

eating
the inside of a human nose.

•

There are as many songs in the world
as branches of coral.

The sponges
the sea pens,

the whips,
have a bloody

earthy smell.
I lay the few I've collected

on a wicker table to dry
under the adonidia palms

and squeeze out the remaining brine.
Soon they begin to sigh.

•

These hours
when the sky is white

my heart reels
like a cay in a squall

and I arrive again
at the scowl

of the redbrick gate.
There were no clouds

that day, above the camp.
The grassy fields

bright green.
Tall birches

in full leaf.
I walked weightlessly

on the train tracks,
one foot

in front of the other
balancing on rails.

I pulled a rusty hair pin
from the soil

put it in my mouth—
75-year-old tarnish

a perfumed
female essence.

The remaining brick
chimneys crumbling,

splintered garrisons—
burial pits moaned—

here was an endless landscape
of hatred this primeval—

it was as if I saw
each soul

who had arrived and
departed,

shimmering,
impossibly,

in the emerald fields.
And everything

broke open
and sang.
•

There were no clouds
that day

I visited Birkenau,
but the sky,

it was white.
The meadows,

they glistened,
the tall birches

beckoned.
Before I left

I ate a few blades of grass—
peeled off a strip of bark,

pressed two sharp stones
into my well-made shoe.

Jacqueline Johnson

Wild Life

It's midnight
and some bird,
some damn bird,
maybe from South America
or Neruda's front porch,
thinks my half-dead, Japanese
red leaf tree
is his paradise.
Sings loves songs
all night long.

Taylor Johnson

Consider the Deer

Consider the deer who, when I say *deer,* doesn't know
whether or not I mean a single one, though there were two
dead and shiny with maggots on the side of the highway;
or, a group of them, always a bit lost
in the divided woods (blame our need to reach
or leave each other, faster).

Consider the deer that I saw dead
on the shoulder, midday midautumn,
whose neck in post–rigor mortis pining
broke itself again so that the head could face
the woods, the woods setting itself alight.
Oh, that I could turn and live again, the deer might say,
recalling that one poet singing to himself, ruining the grass.

Consider that the deer, when called, won't come alone
purely due to linguistic vagary. Who, like me, resists
the gesture toward singularity.
Call my name and the whole woods
rise up inside me. I is a plural state
of being. Consider the multitude
before my footfall; how I'm able to crane my neck back,
see only myself.

from Hymn

Song in secret, Song of spite and
spirit, Song in the temple, temple of Song
and perpetual farewell. Sudden, O
Song, fallen on me as a passing wind,
naming as the wind names—absence, farewell.

O Shadow Song, whose hill is green and leaving,
right my walk in glory, begin.

When the trees were leafless, I put my voice,
O Tenuous Air, among the barren places, among even the
nothingness of frost. Thinking I knew myself. O Fortifier,
O Hidden-in-the-weeds, going green. A green concert, hollow green.

O Ship, your going on without me is my résumé entire.
Thy keel floats on, O Possibility. If I anchor as you.
If I set my anchor here. If I can hum through.
The necessary masterpiece. If I can respond in kind
to the loneliness of Wyeth's *Grape Wine*, recognizing, turning the corner
in the great museum, that I am the drifter, O River,
with his back turned to his fashioner.

How long had I suffered, white-knuckled, anchored to my name, wanting
clearly to walk to the wide avenues wearing ornate buttons, wishing to
be loved by the god of syntax. Had gone mad and gone, tonguing out
my name. This nothingness, I'd proved it upon my pulse. Realized the
self was daily. One moment into the next, as turning the corner I expect
everyone I've known to appear with my other name, a coin in the mouth,
a rotten tooth. As if I'm nothing when not regarded, as light is, as is the
ancient tongue buried below perceivable language, its many tessellations
into sound. *I want to be called as you call yourself*, I say to the unfolding
blooms. How they hold perfection and not announce. Do not announce
on the wide avenues, the mountain's grandeur. The bloom takes part
in the mountain. The mountain is my true lover who, before the road,
humbles me when I set out trying to know. To understand what is below
knowing. Love the mountain. Whose blue face I rise toward, who does
not betray, who is mist-clothed, whose water I gather as breathing.
Who has been one tree. Who has been a seed. Who stills itself in battle.
Who cannot ask, "if then thou gavest." Whose oath to the bloom is
unreachable. O Joiner, let me among that private communion. Let me be
all as if I had all.

Release me, O Redeemer, from the tyranny of my desire
for that which has been weighed against, has killed my people.

Place in my path, O Architect,
the bitter green medicine that reaches for me,

that leans as I do toward the sun,
that huddles together as my people in praise of you,

your name—a sharp taste in my mouth, a righteous sound
I can lean against. O Transformer, whose blessings multiply
before me as yarrow by the train tracks. I trust in

the givenness of things. I trust in the wind and the ache in my knee.
For it is thy hum at my center. O Witness, that breathes me.

Ever Jones

Overheard from the Field

a raindrop pearling itself, a rivulet, tiny stream, the slow unfurling of
enunciation saying
open to the knotted root, underground lightbulb, annual prophet,
lightbearer, sinewy
crone asking the question of the question—*what was it*, that *itness,*
witness of stored history, carbon and oxide tunnels in mycelium's
thickets—that *it*

of hereness unzipping, staying awhile, easing into sway of herd
migration, deer halt,
human pressed into plots making room for us, never who's *the right fit,*
never not-you,
always rain harmony, the seed knocking about, itness spreading into it
all, lashing
nothing, breaking only itself, water knots loosened in mitosis, that itch
of becoming

before the body, before nose presses, before hoof dangles for the first
time in air, and
just like that the underground is ground, the mud-rich body meets
a harvest
of thorns, spells, weeds, enumerative accumulation
of humid language, miner-
al locust, silt spill—the meeting to be, to be here, not the meeting room
but the room

of converging utterance, of stalk, wind language—see the cherry
blossom snow the
almost crops, they are weathering, are weather, their maps are useless
here, inclined toward
nothing, lines unlined, the raindrop heard this, kept going, far from field,
a river held *it,*
it was held, this one seizure, fossilized into nowhere, maybe into a god,
can you

name it, does a name give meaning to your life—the field says *listen,*
the stars unshutter
themselves into being as the hawk recedes into the recesses of branches,
the recession
of what is known, what you know, do you know it, or has dusk opened
another question,
raising its hand, slowly at first, shy thing, tender child, then a blooming
umbrella

of consolation meeting every point at once all that was ever gathered
and lost—this meeting
is adjourned, they say, let's tally the votes, click click click, we are
disinclined, finished
for the day, they say, a column of tanks, they say, refugee corridors, they
say, they say denounce,
they renounce, what does the field say of humanity's disappointing
evolution, so close

to revolution, but the road less traveled, it says, the road to nowhere
untraveled though
constellating between us, a connect-the-dots of interdependence, an
etch-a-sketch
of intersections, circumlocutions, sift shake shake-away the pattern, the
screen a field,
you see, the screen is a field to break upon.

Kasey Jueds

The Vultures

what if it were not distant   that place
     that birthed me   that seemed far even

as we walked there   where the pale seam of trail
     divided the marsh   and the mineral air

thrummed my nape   where behind us
     and out of sight   the vultures

settled on the car   plucking with their beaks
     at every soft part   it offered up

to sky   the wiper blades   the rubber strips
     that sealed the windows   and made   for a while

a kind of safety   a closed box
     of cautious breath   only afterward

we saw the sign   *vultures may damage*
     then the other words   I can't recall

only much later   I remembered
     how the marsh grass swayed   like something

in love   each cluster of stems
     tethered   to the next

by rhizomes and roots   beneath the peaty soil
     so there could be   no telling   one plant

from another   no telling any
     beginning   or end   the marsh

placed all things   side by side
     grass   grass   white lily   fish

a history   of fire-scorch   and flood
     the word *disaster*   held too long

in my mouth   what if I
    were constant   not so tired

of being born   could I find them again
    those birds   as they appeared

when we neared the car   unafraid
    they turned   their faces toward us

and only at the last   as we stepped
    very close to them   flew

Joan Naviyuk Kane

To List

Uaałukitaaq: the boat rocks back and forth over the waters
   as they rise and the land recedes from sight.
       Uaałukitaaq. Utiguliqpin?

The land where women bleed all the time.
   I am homesick. If anything lives at all,
     pests thrive, thronged with men

who are mean to their mothers
   in a tract of moss and stubble.
     Utiguliqtuŋa. Motherless

trouble: our girls never sleep. A land
   where we need no cradle. The soil from which
     the leaves grow large and we do not know why,

we grow large and do not grow back.
   The grown leave and do not go back,
     the gone grow and do not go back.

Are you homesick?
   Am I going to go back?

Darker Passage

It has been bound with rope
& the weapons of a child

     this land with its laws
     serving as wire & root

to bind us together Sinew snare the unseen growth
of the green tree many rivers south whose stump now shoals into use

The wire itself works its way through layer upon layer
of land submerged of ice of ash though lakes would
be the eyes of the earth   A phreatomagmatic blue sprawl the Devil

Mountain maar   The Imuruk Basin drains through inland veins
scrawling tributaries in familiar names The giant granite tors
at Serpentine (*Iyat*, the cooking pot) sentineled in unscoured
stone towering endlessly into the flickering sky

            Auksruaq

     like the blood that seeps across America in such hot & dim &
strenuous times where one still cannot be serene Red phalarope: might we
follow, leaving the meadow wet with tears? From next to fledge & then
to move again right out to sea circling
      pent
vortices to upwell food Let us lose our grief
in great rafts as we translate the renamed straits

Our limb
Our burnt and broken

           At last make noise of a truth
together. At length let us return to furrow

              furrows

where we made portage with our boats

             Let us keep

the line taut we could not **cede** the land with his hands
at our throat his face betraying a dream a possession

He lost but

a hound   a horse & a dove in his seizure of
we bereavers
bereft   reaved of & in it

Julia Spicher Kasdorf

A Mother Near the West Virginia Line Considers the Public Health

The industry thinks I'm too dumb to back down; they don't know
I do this for my mom and dad. They were sixty-nine and seventy-one.

He had pulmonary fibrosis, worked with asbestos all his life. She grew up
near the coke ovens back when kids were sent into the mines to pick coal.

So they both had lung problems, but their home, the next holla over,
sits 350 feet from a compressor station. We sealed the house,

set up an air scrubber, but—four of their neighbors passed last year, too.

*

We bought the coal rights to our 115 acres because we know
the company will come up to your front door, but we let the gas rights go,

just didn't see this coming. A gentleman from New Jersey leased our
    land.
One day we come home to find pink ribbons tied in the field. Then
    bulldozers.

They put in four shallow wells and a Marcellus well on a five-acre pad
    seven hundred feet
from our porch. The workers come in by the busload. All those strangers

on our land, 24/7, could have been rapists or pedophiles. For about a year
they didn't have a Port-a-John. I looked out my window one morning

to a guy peeing in the driveway. The dog brought in used toilet paper.
The workers have to be young, strong. Kids in trucks twelve to sixteen
    hours a day,

that should be placarded "hazardous waste." They live on junk food;
I know because we picked up the wrappers. Then our dog disappeared.

We saw Sara's tracks in the snow go right up to the well pad.

*

When crayfish died in our spring, we knew the methane had migrated.
Now you can light it on fire. Our neighbor put in a water line; we guessed

their well had gone bad and they'd settled, but they paid for it themselves.
We had water buffalos two years before we paid to run a line in from the
    road.

When they laid the gas pipeline, those big trucks drove over our waterline
and busted it up. When I hollered at the drivers, I got dragged into court,

me and our son, four years old then, both got an injunction.
They tried to say I'm an unfit mother, too, but the judge wouldn't hear it.

I look at pictures of my little one from that time, and he has the same
    dark circles
under his eyes as the Hallowich kids. He'd get terrible stomach pains,
    nothing

we could do but hold him. My older boy had the nosebleeds and rashes.
I couldn't keep him inside all the time. I'll show you pictures. If you speak
    up,

you get more security. We had guards here 24/7, armed and unlicensed
in Pennsylvania. They got real interested in my walks down by the crick.

One asked me, What do you do down there in the evening? I said, I walk
and I have pawpaw trees, want to come along? He could have used

the exercise, so he walked with us, and I got to know the night guard.
His mom was sick the same time mine was. We're still in touch on
    Facebook.

*

They drilled the gas pipeline on a weekend, didn't go where the DEP said,
so it blew out in our crick—bentonite and "residual waste" clouding

clean water stocked with trout. That's when I cried. That crick flows
into the Mon, and people get their drinking water out of that river.

Another side effect of the drilling no one thinks about it all the swearing.
And it's not just the men.

*

"Alternate waste disposal on site" means they can bury radioactive
drill cuttings in your land. When they drained the frack pits,

they shook the tarp and bulldozed the sludge into the ground, too.
There's places we mow now, but we don't feed that hay to our horses.

I can't dig or plant a post there. Why don't they tell us
not to grow food or let beef graze back there?

The stock sale registers animals now, so if I sell hay to a neighbor,
he sells his steer, and someone's sick from the meat, that comes back on me.

*

People collect royalties on this well a mile away. We just care for the place
and pay taxes. The well tenders come about once a week

to the shallow wells and every day to the Marcellus. Two or three
times a week water trucks come in here and draw brine, and every two
   weeks

they blow it down, so whatever's on the line goes into the air.
Once the brine tank vented for forty-five minutes. My horse's eyes
   swelled shut,

and one went blind. They've had the nosebleeds. There's a big gum tree
near the well that loses its leaves in the middle of summer.

*

We saw clouds of silica sand blow off train cars over the little league field,
and someone was holding a newborn there with us in the stands.

When I complained about them parking silica trains by the elementary
   school,
the gentleman said, "It's just sand; your kids play in it."

*

We didn't have internet before this, but you have to follow the permits
because the industry tells you nothing. You have to go to the courthouse

and pull your file, and when you find out what they did to your land,
you're just sick. Let them think I'm too dumb to back down. My son

won't play on any T-ball team with industry logos on their shirts.

Athena Kildegaard

Sudden

Flesh is not annihilated but fulfilled.
— NAN SHEPHERD

I pull weeds I have no name for,
pile them, roots together,
in the blue wheelbarrow.
Fires from the north alter our weather,
the sky's the color of iron ore.

It is hard to breathe the thick air
and my scalp sweats, but I
am light and agile, all spare
strength, as if I'd come by
my body only today, as if here

at the farm, wetland to the east,
lake to the west, a turkey hen and her eight
chicks, an eastern kingbird, a feast
of tomatoes coming on, a wren's mate
with three gold straws in his beak,

the list can go on, leopard frogs, all
morning a hummingbird in the hollyhocks,
garter snakes swerving, the lone call
of a loon, a deer huffing in the oaks—
as if here I am suddenly, wonderfully small.

Grant Kittrell

the plan was to build the pipeline   through my left lung

i was standing in the way   someone said
it will cause irreversible   damage to the environment
by which they meant   i might not love again
faith is in the body   and it is only there
i used to love so much   more and so much less
in the photograph folks   are backpacking over the ridge
of my alveoli to where a rib   bone will soon be cut and it tickles
and feels something like faith   but is only hope I think which
might be enough we'll see   if you stand folks in a long line
and shoot straight down it   the bullet will eventually stop
in someone there will   always be a final loss though ours
might be shuddering from   some other green planet where
the resource is pumped   through a pipe by which since
we've started talking   we've all been bound
in flesh yours to mine   mine to hers hers
to the Great Valley   where we lie tangled
in the bedsheets   and though our breaths
are short these days   some still say love lies
in the heart and it might   still in any case
there is already at least   one pipe in there

                    and it is doing what it can
                    and it is not enough
                    and it is doing just fine

Sophie Klahr

Tender

I spent late morning weeping with the news:

a black bear with burnt paws is euthanized

along the latest wildfire's newest edge.

It was crawling on its forearms, seeking

a place to rest. I google more; reports

leak out: the bear had bedded down behind

a house, below a pine, to lick its paws.

In hours before its end, officials named

it Tenderfoot, though some reports report

just Tender. Later, I will teach a class

where we'll discuss the lengths of lines in poems.

I'll say a sonnet is a little song

to hold a thing that otherwise cannot

be held: a lonely thing; a death; a bear.

Christopher Kondrich

Endling

When the second-to-last of a species dies, the last
becomes what is called an *endling*,

a term that means the beginning
of us caring about it. Whereas, when the last

of a species dies, it takes terminology with it,
the syntax of us seeing it, the red grammar of its wounds,

the ellipsis on the bare branch it would return to
later, sooner than we'd think.

The last of a species also takes its accent—
an act, a scent specific to its touch,

the trace amounts of oils from its feathers or fur
it would leave on our skin, so that what we would smell

was not us, but the smell of that species having left
some of its body on ours. Not anywhere, but here

on my hand, this palm, this place
where the base of my fingers meets my palm

like the mouths of five rivers meeting the same ocean,
which can still be where I held it whenever I remember,

but memory is no landscape
for a species to live. Not any. Not my own.

Brandon Krieg

Invasives

High tide pressed me
up into
      the yellow, invasive
Scotch broom

whose roots hold fast this
crumbling cliff.

Against root-give, I clung
      ever more urgently to the *still,*
small voice—whose seeds

blew into me from 19c fields—
watching tankers drag

coal hillsides, tourist districts, shining decks
of cars past
      distant peaks,

and since this tide would not
retreat,
cut a hard path up the cliff,
made my way through vacationers

sauntering the green of a fin de siècle
fort. Where genteel, sympathetic

            murder was taught,
in haphazard rows,
children at art camp lounged with ice creams,

laughing avidly. There must be a real
higher or harder
than this, I said,

and took the trail up to a bluff overlooking
international waters,

walked the rim of the impregnable
concrete walls of the abandoned

gun emplacements. This is a place, finally,

nothing can invade,
I thought—admiring

the Mayan-monumentality
stripped

of deity—I can build hard
apprehension here.

Up a narrow ladder, I climbed
into the watchtower,

shut the iron visor, and
sat in ammonia-smelling dark

where *deep* and *calm* and *perpetual*
could never take.

Then Japanese fire-balloons
floated elegantly

past the long-range guns
in this afterimage

of a state-park plaque, touching down
70 years ago
in Montana forests, igniting
a recent candidate's promise

of colonies on the moon.

Petra Kuppers

Found on the Pond Deck

The husk of a tiny dragonfly, translucent,
clings upside down on a yellow spear of grass
its roots clasp the dry wood of the deck.
Tiny white fibers everywhere: the planks, breathing,
expectorate their innards, wood weeps and uncoils
what it knew when it stood, tall in a wet redwood forest,
before the chains of a truckbed, dark and long, bite, here,
where all trees are twisted into themselves against
the prevailing winds. On that white-spun deck,
I remember my watery nature, pour my liquid body
to wash away the pain of the shorter years,
to wash away the pain of a hollow embrace,
the feeling that we all will slide, not into the clear pool,
but into the murk of a place that should not be settled.

Found on Mushrooming Walk

Wow, footprint sucker, very flowery chemical
vein not quite in marble.
Old warm sea. Old times. Oh you are so delicate.
You cling on, don't you, beneath the dust of meteorite bowl,
hesitant tentacle preserved and unveiled, immodest,
to the newbies, twinkle mushroom feeds
on air and last night's rain,
pinhead knows nothing of exoskeletal growing pain, rub of dust
on skin chafed by sunburn and the wind's whip.
Stem too delicate to
be picked, a tight little cap peeks for a day at the first hungry bird
without a mushrooming book, extravagant spores ride high
out over the mountain. So, you will live.
Hitch up on boot, dust the sock, lodge yourself,
soar stuck on the windy desert rim, flat stony face.

Joe M. Lamb

Trinity

I am an old man wading the Trinity River, fishing in a snowstorm, the river pushing against my thighs, my wading staff vibrating in the current.

I am a fisherman fishing to be caught, caught by the hummingbird's fierce flight in the blowing flakes, caught by the snow on the pine branch arranged as in a Japanese woodcut, caught by the green seam beneath the alder trees where the river deepens, dark with the promise of steelhead.

I fish to let the beauty of the place wash over me like a wave.

I fish to remember that I am a little ocean, some bones and gristle, but mostly water, grateful that my skin makes a place where water finds its thoughts.

I am an old man wading Trinity River, wondering what I will leave on the shore. I am an old man bowing to the river, offering apologies for our sins against water. I am an old man preaching to himself that our sins against water are sins against our selves. I am an old man preaching to himself that all living beings—old man, hummingbird, alder tree, steelhead trout—are water flowing to the sea. I am an old man fishing to remember that water need not fear the sea.

10,000 casts and not a single bite. Lucky me. Such joy in not catching and in being caught.

John Lane

Elegy for Sugar Sand and Slash Pine

Feet above sea level five miles
out Cape San Blas, at low tide.

"This strand will be underwater
in fifty years," Betsy said earlier

at breakfast, our B&B fellow
guests nodding in agreement,

then adding their home range too,
Philly, another coastal hotspot

with city charter that would be
voided in a geologic minute

by sea level rise. Today
seems at least superficially

a beauty, yellow butterflies,
a few migrating monarchs,

a ubiquitous osprey fishing
the shallow channel behind

the beach. But the old normal
is not the new normal,

instead, every glacier calves
oblivion. We ascend twenty-foot

dunes at the state park, built up
by prevailing winds and tides.

A woman huffs up from the gravel
parking lot, complains, "You

pay for this view." Her husband,
tan as a vanilla wafer, stalls

before he can see the Gulf,
his plastic Crocs filled

with sand like concrete
overshoes. When I achieve

the dune line's last summit
I feel surprisingly dystopic—

before me, Cormac McCarthy's
final scene in *The Road*,

a barren empty shore,
a sliver of sugar sand,

and slash pine, a few
sharp blades of palmetto,

a raw ocean to the horizon's
end. All that's missing is

the beached plundered tanker
and the petroleum smell

of apocalypse. I watch a swarm
of dragonflies like black drones

buzz the terrain, nothing hurried
about their tactics. Last night

we ate crabs safe in their dark
pot of seawater until it boiled.

J. Drew Lanham

from Bird Watching: Four Poems for Dead Negroes

[2. WHAT THE STARLING SAID]

The starling,
meanwhile
more American than most on two legs
but without benefit of a hyphen
to prove cross-continental citizenship
Sat high on a streaming cable
mellow buzzed
off Loud Bud
cloud upward wafting
Lines sagged cutting catty-corner between
what was 38th and Chicago Ave—
soon to be named for the human
no longer in existence—
shook its yellow-beaked head
unbelieving
reshuffled spangles
    on immigrant iridescence
knowing the status
of being neither
served nor protected by law
gifted benefit of doubt
or common decency,
and subject therefore
to the
same suffocating ends
as the corpse
lain crumpled in the street,
before whatever little "g" gods
watch over dark-hued beings,
let loose proclamation
that rose above the din

to more metal on metal raged screech
than smooth practiced speech,
before joining the evening
murmuration in protest.
Sturnus vulgaris,
neither profane nor dirty
kept vigil,
sat murmuring
to the flock gathered to watch
organized by empathy on the issue
of whose existences mattered.
Clearly
that black life
        did not.

[3. WHY THE WHIP-POOR-WILL WEPT]

Meanwhile, in Louisville, KY
a whip-poor-will in the park
a rarity now for those particular parts
sang in the black night
as she slept.
The darkness creased soft
around its name-calling
shaped as if caressing each note that fell
from its broad-gaped goatsucker mouth.
The great owl heard.
Raised tufted horns
spun its head round almost to completion
blinked. Nodded.
Hooted in between the Caprimulgids
syncopating 2 and 4.
Almost a hybrid cross of communication
between Miles and a Brubeck-ian 5/4
A nighthawk pierced the streetlamp's glow
Staccato peents announcing the unseen
between the owl's genuflection
and the whip-poor-will's cry.
Its peenting seemed percussive
A snare drum beating taps

on the edge of something tight.
They all knew when
the harsh knocks *didn't* come
and the nine-millimeter shots popped off
in the still of that night,
she would not wake up past
their own crepuscular being.
Night, they knew, was for living
but for Breonna lying fast asleep
dying.

Deborah Leipziger

Lobo

*for Paulo Paulino Guajajara, known as Lobo, who was a
"Guardian of the Amazon," killed by illegal loggers*

I guard the forest
its canopy of reflected stars
the morpho butterflies, blue moons
parakeets, bromelias, the fish
the roots of trees
drinking in the river

I guard the forest
the children of the tribe

I guard the canopy with its toucans, parakeets
emerald.
I guard the forest floor, with its snakes
I guard the mating jaguars

I knew
they would kill me.
I could not have imagined
that it would be a shot to the
face   that my body would be
left, in the forest

Now
You guard the forest,
its canopy of reflected stars
the morpho butterflies, the blue moons
parakeets, bromelias, the fish
the roots of trees
drinking in the river

You guard the forest
the children of the tribe

You guard the canopy with its toucans, parakeets
emerald
The forest floor
The mating jaguars

Julia Levine

Milk

Even in the dream, it is long past the possible
when I uncover my breast and hold the baby
close enough to drink. How helpless he is

to resist, helpless as the mind in a deep dream
to stop and change direction. Though, on waking,
the mind remembers our grown daughters

and the room where we sleep, and beyond it,
the outside made white with smoke from a fire.
Remembers yesterday's eerie, milk-gold light

we walked through, and stopped a moment
beside a baby fox. In the road, wasps lit on his skull,
their black bodies beading his torn-apart torso,

while gnats and flies sipped at the glistening.
And the work of those winged things seemed a fire
chewing through manzanita and alder,

Douglas fir and cedar; the maggots and flies
and wasps carrying the forest out of the fox,
the way the fire carried the forest out of the world.

You asked then if a mother fox could feel sadness.
And because last night my mind had used a memory
of my body to deceive me, had pressed my son close,

believing if he drank, I could keep him, today
I want to believe the dead fox was a twin,
a mirror image following behind the vixen,

the way a dream can shadow the mind,
and the mind helpless against our stillborn son
that lives inside my dreams and runs silent

as a wild fox behind our daughters. It was dusk
when we turned to go, so quickly the wasps and flies
rose together, as if the black and yellow robes

they carried through the milk-gold light had slipped
from the death they had just been covering. All of us helpless
against the beauty of the hurt world as it burns.

Rossy Lima

Water Path / Aguacamino

Let me gather the river with my hands
to guard it in my mouth,
may its current open a path for me
in the loneliness of silence.

That the cylinders which rise
like a blister on the shore
be a panpipe that praises the condor
and if the condor has been forgotten
may my wings be the shade that caresses both nations.

May the abandoned house in the south
never put out its flare,
I can see the smoke of nostalgia
from this new land,
from the water path.

The smoke brings butterflies every year,
and my heart follows them
yelling *Papalotzin* till I wake up.

Between the ground and sky
may my body always be a border,
let my tears stop being tears,
let these eyes cease being eyes,
      let them be wide and traveling mirrors.

Que pueda recoger el río con mis manos
para guardarlo en mi boca,
que su corriente me abra camino
en la soledad del silencio.

Que los cilindros que se levantan
como una llaga en la orilla
sean una zampoña que alabe al cóndor,
y que si se ha olvidado al cóndor
mis alas sean la sombra que acaricia las dos patrias.

Que la casa abandonada en el sur
nunca apague su antorcha,
desde la nueva tierra alcanzo a ver
el humo de la nostalgia,
del aguacamino.

Ese humo trae mariposas cada año,
y mi corazón las sigue
gritando *Papalotzin* hasta que despierto.

Que por entre el suelo y el aire
mi cuerpo sea siempre frontera,
que mi lágrima deje de ser lágrima,
que estos ojos dejen de ser ojos,
     que sean espejos anchos y viajeros.

Ada Limón

Drowning Creek

Past the strip malls and the power plants,
out of the holler, past Gun Bottom Road
and Brassfield and before Red Lick Creek,
there's a stream called Drowning Creek where
I saw the prettiest bird I'd seen all year,
the belted kingfisher, crested in its Aegean
blue plumage, perched not on a high snag
but on a transmission wire, eyeing the creek
for crayfish, tadpoles, and minnows. We were
driving fast toward home and already our minds
were pulled taut like a high black wire latched
to a utility pole. I wanted to stop, stop the car
to take a closer look at the solitary, stocky water
bird with its blue crown and its blue chest
and its uncommonness. But already we were
a blur and miles beyond the flying fisher
by the time I had realized what I'd witnessed.
People were nothing to that bird, hovering over
the creek. I was nothing to that bird, which wasn't
concerned with history's bloody battles or why
this creek was called Drowning Creek, a name
I love though it gives me shivers, because
it sounds like an order, a place where one
goes to drown. The bird doesn't call the creek
that name. The bird doesn't call it anything.
I'm almost certain, though I am certain
of nothing. There is a solitude in this world
I cannot pierce. I would die for it.

The Carrying

The sky's white with November's teeth,
and the air is ash and woodsmoke.
A flush of color from the dying tree,
a cargo train speeding through, and there,
that's me, standing in the wintering
grass watching the dog suffer the cold
leaves. I'm not large from this distance,
just a fence post, a hedge of holly.
Wider still, beyond the rumble of overpass,
mares look for what's left of green
in the pasture, a few weanlings kick
out, and theirs is the same sky, white
like a calm flag of surrender pulled taut.
A few farms over, there's our mare,
her belly barrel-round with foal, or idea
of foal. It's Kentucky, late fall, and any
mare worth her salt is carrying the next
potential stake's winner. Ours, her coat
thicker with the season's muck, leans against
the black fence and this image is heavy
within me. How my own body, empty,
clean of secrets, knows how to carry her,
knows we were all meant for something.

Layli Long Soldier

Steady Summer

solstice grasses
see this one's a natural
anesthetic he said
when they fast
they cannot food
careful water so slide
grass needle tips
around the edges
of wounds this summer
potent
grass songs
a grass chorus moves *shhhhh*
through half-propped
windows I swallow
grass scent the solstice
makes a mind
wide makes it
oceanic blue a field in crests
swirling gyres the moving
surface fastened
in June light
here I'm certain
that certain
kinds of talk
only = pain excusing
myself I paddle
deep in high
grass waves I'm safer
outdoors than in / in those
heady grasses the mouth
loosens confesses
I don't trust nobody
     but the land I said

I don't mean
present company
of course
you understand the grasses
hear me too always
present the grasses
confident grasses polite
command to *shhhhh*
shhh listen

      at the bottom of trailer steps
      grasshoppers power up
      plate bodies jet wings
      knock knock high
      speed thru a swaying
      green page single-spaced
      blades bold hollow
      stems *air italics*

               shhhhh

                      in midday open
                      two horseflies love-buzz
                      a simple humid meeting
                      motorized sex in place
                      then loose again
                      infinite circle eights

      shhhhh   *listen*

                     down the path
                     Auntie steps onto the porch
                     the dog pads across wood planks
                     a pause to nudge her foot

                             ssshhh

in my thoughts I hear her
two states away ask for more
mac n cheese this is good Dad
my favorite   their forks click
in blue gardens flowered borders
scrubbed secondhand plates

shhhh

        this grass*shhhh*

   shhhh

            who have I become

from Whereas

WHEREAS I did not desire in childhood to be a part of this but desired most of all to be a part. A piece combined with others to make up a whole. Some but not all of something. In Lakota it's haŋké, a piece or part of anything. Like the creek trickling behind my aunt's house where Uncle built her a bridge to cross from bank to bank, not far from a grassy clearing with three tipis, a place to gather. She holds three-day workshops on traditional arts, young people from Kyle and Potato Creek arrive one by one eager to *parti*cipate. They have the option my auntie says to sleep at home and return in the morning but by and large they'll stay and camp even during South Dakota winters. The comfort of being together. I think of Plains winds snowdrifts ice and limbs the exposure and when I slide my arms into a wool coat and put my hand to the doorknob, ready to brave the sub-zero dark, someone says be careful out there always consider the snow your friend. Think badly of it, snow will burn you. I walk out remembering that for millennia we have called ourselves Lakota meaning friend or ally. This relationship to the other. Some but not all, still our piece to everything;

Whereas Native People are [   ] people with a deep and abiding [   ] in the [   ], and for millennia Native Peoples have maintained a powerful [   ] connection to this land, as evidenced by their [   ] and legends;

•

Whereas the Federal Government condemned the [   ], [   ], and [   ] of Native Peoples and endeavored to as-similate them by such policies as the redistribution of land under the Act of February 8, 1887 (25 U.S.C. 331; 24 Stat. 388, chap-ter 119) (commonly known as the "General Allotment Act"), and the forcible removal of Native [   ] from their [   ] to faraway boarding schools where their Native [   ] and [   ] were degraded and forbidden;

Sandy Longhorn

The Crumple Zone

Pinnacle Mountain State Park, June 12, 2023

Signs call it a mountain at a thousand feet
above sea level and my mind drifts back
to Colorado, days spent selling topo maps
of fourteeners, living in the sweeping
purple shadow of Pikes Peak. We wore
shirts that claimed "Don't trust anyone under
14,000 feet" and judged the tourists' boots.
Thirty years on, long since rooted here
in Arkansas, I wonder who gets to name
a mountain *mountain* anyway?

Here at the eastern edge of the Ouachitas,
land created in the crumple zone of two plates
colliding, force as strong as what formed those
Rocky Mountain majesties, just older, I stand
on the still aftermath of dramatic folding and faulting.
Beneath my feet, echoes of upheaval sing
through the jackfork stone and the grappling hook
roots of hardwoods, the hickories and the oaks.
Around me the views shift from sweeping vistas
to the closed-in green of the trails.

I hike the RVT over to the East Quarry Spur,
as a chorus of birdsong tracks my path.
Today, the eastern wood-pewee is new
to me and I pause to cement that song
in memory until a long train whistle
from the Union Pacific interrupts,
spurs my feet onward. I spot a nurse log
decked out in resurrection fern, each green
frond rooted deep in dying bark, a spider's
web running like a tripwire from an upthrust
branch down to the parsley hawthorn at my feet—

everything alive and breathing in this preserved
green abundance.

Name it what you will, judge it small,
a hill in comparison. My knees still feel the ache
of pulling against gravity, of heaving this aging body
up the path, and when the trail turns onto a lookout,
language drops away just the same.

Éireann Lorsung

Garden cycle (keeping time)

Early blue lavender ("Munstead") and air cannons over grainfields
(the pheasant, visiting us regularly now, startles in the hedges)

Rosemary flowers like minuscule orchids (and insects see how to go)
Writing at all feels pointless from the moment one realizes about death

—all the marigolds are coming up now, just as I thought they would

Cosmos and marigold
cosmos and marigold—and next to them
hyssop, scenting the floors of the ninth century

> One point of close attention
> is to see that things are not
> dead, despite appearances

> > Blood and chive flowers
> > the thing *flowers* and then *dies*
> > the cat biting the rabbit's carotid artery

A red poppy / a pink poppy

> > all of everything opening
> > with a cross in the middle

> I get preoccupied with my vegetables
> to distract myself from the pain in my lung

and hate the ant and the aphid
> as dry weather brings the cabbages to bolt

> (berry on its bed of
> > straw; bee-
> balm)
> > (a cuckoo,
> > > a few
> > thistles)

"The book attempts to stave off the single end"

A honeybee fumbles
itself through air
and *is* more itself
without question
than I am myself

    —although I do not know
    whether it knows it can die

Mint takes over
horsetails take over
creeping ranunculus
takes over thistles
take over; *one day*
and the human
disappears

        Only anemone
        Don't worry

     "Flowers cannot understand"

        The rose goes down
        to the green siphons
        on its youngest leaves.

        Does being able
        to name it
        make death more
        terrifying or less?

—If I begin
to misplace words—   the chitchit
               of birdspeak

    for language now

Lea Marshall

Future Folk Tales: Fox

They walked all day with a thin fox
as their companion. He carried his tail
easily over the stones and they admired
his face like a delicate chisel.

Toward evening he turned to them
and said, I cannot stay with you but
since you are the last one on earth
I will tell you my secrets. And so

for one hundred evenings he spoke
and his secrets wove slow vines
among their ribs, around their lungs
and by the end they understood

willow branches and leaf rot, rabbits'
terror, the slow hammer of roots
through concrete, their own heart—
the deathly intertwining of desire

and waste. Wind rattled past
the fox was gone, they thought,
until they heard the lost violin
of his voice threading the hills

with them as they walked gently
on new grass and with relief
left hope behind.

Future Folk Tales: Fireflies

Somehow the fireflies still
emerged that summer, still
hovered and would alight,
gently curious, on his outstretched
hands—they felt soft as a tiny purr,
listening antennae and blurred wings,
though not as many as before.
Don't mistake us for innocence,
they said, constellating on a thundery
evening. We know the dark and we string
it through the trees you left behind.

Jennifer Martelli

Snakes

I have to learn to breathe differently, here,

Las Vegas–style. Today, I'll tour the Strip

and all the ways my diamondback snake

brain could unhinge and fix: blackjack, cool

green menthol cigarettes, shrimp curved

in pain on ice sculpted into the Pietà.

I ask my friend, whom I've loved

longer than my husband or my children,

about snakes. I've done my research:

colubridae, Mojave green, sidewinder,

coachwhip, panamint rattler, basin green.

Will they come to the blue warm pool

she dug out back, surrounded by brush

and cacti blooms, herbs? No, she said,

only baby scorpions come. Clear and small

as my fingertip, all crustacean, arachnid

and clawed. She says I may get a nosebleed

because of the heat, the arid air, the strange

elevation of a city so deep in its dry basin.

Airea D. Matthews

His Eye on the Sparrow

after hanif

I guess black people can write about flowers at a time like this
since every poem turns on itself. Starts one way to end
another. We see it in nature too. How seed turns to
leaf regardless of its earth or the thought inside my head
blossoms into a hyacinth with as sweet a scent. Even in
d r e a m s ,   t h o u g h t ' s   p r e t e n d   c o u s i n ,   I   o f t e n
see Mamie Till. She walks the church aisle toward
her son's body while wisteria bloats the casket's brim and papered
b   o   u   g   a   i   n   v   i   l   l   e   a   b   r   a   c   t   s
emerge from where his eye once was. An entire garden
from the nutrients of once human. And not to mention
all those awed birds that circle Emmett's pillowed corpse.
So many in the tabernacle. Not predators of the fleshly bloom or
harbingers of his God's descent, not refugees fleeing his exilic
b   o   d   y   b   u   t   e   t   e   r   n   i   t   y   '   s
messengers. We, who pull breath, confuse death's irony. Whoever dies and is
r e m e m b e r e d   s t a y s   l i v i n g .

Janet McAdams

Earthling

That winter, that warm winter, no one

wanted to be ordinary. We sat

on a pile of plastic, threatened as a

farm where the dog is tied up barking.

Land, we meant to say sorry

—we are so sorry—

to the red dirt of your body.

We meant to say meat or dirty water.

We meant to say before our bones became lace

before we had to lean forward to swallow.

You remember how the story goes: We came in peace.

But tell that to a drop of water trying to linger.

Anne Haven McDonnell

Once There Were Fish

Once, the rivers moved both ways, up
        through the one mind of salmon, silvered
into many bodies, sweeping across
        the land like weather. I stood
knee-deep in the last of it, Alaska
        the year the tundra burned,
the year the old ones fell through
        the ice that always held. I saw
an old buck, hook-jawed and mottled,
        sloughing off skin, nosing his weary
way past my shin. Then I saw the river
        turn back its silted face, mumbling
to its darling gravel along the shore.
        The gulls lifted and flung
their white flags, their shrieks tearing
        holes in the rain. I tell you
I saw it as it once was here
        and everywhere—the ground
thundering thousands of hooves,
        wings darking out
the sky, numberless animals
        spreading and gathering like storms.
How salmon carried the sea's longing
        to return. I stood knee-deep
in my own longing, casting
        along the edge of current and slack,
dragging orange yarn tied on a hook
        across their path. And when
the sockeye struck, the yank
        pulled both the oldest
and youngest parts of me. And when
        I pressed my palm on the flank,
that golden eye—cold
        and steady as it stared

where? Shelves of ice sloughing
        into sea, rivers running straight
down the moulins. The rushing
        world, the melt. The fire.
The fish shuddering still
        under my hand.

Inside a lateness, a singing under snow

The pine marten have their oral history
here—long memories of salmon skin
on a pile of sunflower seeds. This one

arrives two winters later to curl
her body, a long ribbon of muscle and fur
in this hanging bucket of birdseed

in first gauzy light. I see that white patch
on her chestnut fur, the pretty darkening
at tips of ears, nose, paws, and tail.

And there, under pillows of snow,
the creek shushes the sharp
architecture of ice. Here, meet

my mother, famous to the pine marten
who drop her secret name in hollow
logs and tunnels under roots under

snow. Here she comes, limping down
the hall on her metal knee, praying
for pine marten to appear. Outside,

beetles carve maps under the skin
of lodgepole, leaving scripts of death
across the forest. There's a tangle

of blow-down impassable now, but not
for the marten who moves like
water unspooling branch to branch

and leaps, leaving fresh tracks
in a clean cursive that means
joy, means fierce, means something

to this forest of rust and gray—
which is not cold enough now to kill
the beetles that swarm the trees,

rubbing violins on their bellies to click
and chirp their war cries. It is
rare to see a marten. But this

one comes to eat this rare fat
and watches warily from the bucket,
as my mother whispers *beauty,*

you, beauty. Because I know so much
is dying, I love this marten
with some desperation, the way

I love my mother and cannot
imagine this world without her. I know
she will die and I will not be

ready. The creek makes a ribbon
of living trees the marten
needs in this mountain of snags.

I don't know where the story goes,
but there's my mother, laying out
a piece of salmon skin again.

And snow keeps falling,
piling higher on living branches
than the skinny dead, but burying

both. Listen, here's the creek singing,
and trees exhaling as they drink.

Rose McLarney

Fresh Tracks

Coywolf: New dog–coyote–wolf hybrid already numbers in the millions

Out of coyote and wolf crossed. Out of coyote's compromises
about where to live, what to hunt. Out of wolf's big bones,
bearing wolf's bulk, fed by wolf's broad jaw, wolf's bite.

Out of dog, out of willingness to mate with dog,
out of tameness turned. Away from coyness. Out of coyness.

Into clamor, crashes of cars and construction, into noise
no longer weapon against the wild. Into crowds, into cities,
not creeping. Holding full tail high, nose proudly low
for the trails to where fat, suburban rabbits go.

Into the unheralded havens of highway sides, into the unclaimed
kingdoms of park corners, into habitats we create
that cannot shelter us—the tender furless. Following graveyards'
green, beckoning glows from borough to borough. Each generation,
gorged on garbage, grows.

From earth, when we can no longer endure or
be endured. From cold forests cut and no more, from trees,
from all we've made fall like the trees. Following timber,
following trade routes, following trains, arriving by railroad,
as once to the West, another civilization—

Out of survival, out of desire for it, out of dogs past being pets
and the doggedness with which life persists
despite the end of one form. Out of the fresh tracks life lays.
Over the ways of we who will not scavenge
so cannot be saved. Street-crossing, side-walking
coywolves, not coy, they come.

—After Philip Levine

Lucien Darjeun Meadows

Violet

Cloud, birdfoot, common blue. Blush in your sex,
Bruise on my chin. Chalk dust and moth wings. Quiet
Under sycamore. My face pressed to bark.
Squish of toes in spring mud. Stillness after.
River rising beside, we hear the call—
More silence than whisper, smell of first rain
Never leaving my palms, tongue. We love like
No other blooming. Never trillium,
Angel's trumpet, beebalm. First spring wind, new
Fuzz on your chin. Slant of light, your long hair,
If only, only, to hold hands walking
Down the dirt road. Somewhere a deeper shade
Of blue. Backs of your knees cup like petals,
Filled with salt. Those long nights of rain, what thirst.

Mile 57—

There was a boy who was a boy who was a tree who was a river and a rock and cloud. Who was a nothing more than a something who wanted to be nothing but a flash under sky over field. Who wanted to be a space between dusk and dark between night and sunrise when the temperature drops before dawn and the ghosts of the hollers come running back to their beds. Who was a breath when he should have been a fist, a kiss when he should have been a kick, some ill-timed sparkle of a boy in his mother's dress, a bruised boy when his father came home early when the mines got too hot to work one summer day. Who stood naked in his changing body out in the grapevines and crushed the long black fruit in his hands, smearing his face in darkness. Who wanted to pass, pass white, pass straight, pass cool, pass normal. Who wanted to remain 59 pounds forever. Who wanted things that could never be named. Not things, people. Who would sleep beside the river, in the crook of the old sycamore, out in a tent of branches and leaves on the game trail. Who hoped, every day, to wake changed into a deer, a good boy. Who wanted to run, and run, and run until he woke up from this dream. Surely this is a dream. Let it be a dream because no one can hear me.

Rajiv Mohabir

Why Whales Are Back in New York City

After a century, humpbacks migrate
again to Queens. They left
due to sewage and white froth

banking the shores from polychlorinated-
biphenyl-dumping into the Hudson
and winnowing menhaden schools.

But now grace, dark bodies
of song return. Go to the seaside—

Hold your breath. Submerge.
A black fluke silhouetted

against the Manhattan skyline.

Now ICE beats doors
down on Liberty Avenue
to deport. I sit alone on orange

A train seats, mouth sparkling
from Singh's, no matter how
white supremacy gathers

at the sidewalks, flows down
the streets, we still beat our drums
wild. Watch their false-god statues

prostrate to black and brown hands.
They won't keep us out
though they send us back.

Our songs will pierce the dark
fathoms. Behold the miracle:

what was once lost now
leaps before you.

Stomach Full of Trash

Put your hand inside
my wound. You stud me
in jewels and now
I am floating in the bay.
With your arms submerged,
pass my pharynx and reach
into my pouch of skin
folded on skin. Pull out
the garbage in my gut,
gleaming as the razor jewels
of empire. Is my plastic
a prophet sent to predict
your doom? The coolie is here
to serve you. Here's the oil
from my head that keeps me
afloat and bloating. Lay on this
palanquin of my ribs
and baleen. I will carry
you on my back. I will dress you
in rhinestones and sequins
scales and you can penetrate
my deep as a mermaid—
half fish and all human
desire for conquest.

Daniela Naomi Molnar

Memory of a larger mind

A glacier is a ghosted god : restless and feral.

A glacier shimmies and bulges, eats whole trees.

A glacier is a hungry lip

shouting lost language as it recedes.

A glacier is a ghost of future ruin.

Inside the glacier

sums water's boundless tally :

zero :

one symbol for the largest

infinity

and the smallest

infinity—both at once, combined.

You / I are ghosts among ghosts inside ghosted gods.

Which is what it's like, now, being alive.

Pray we fail the final ghosting.

Pray the spectacle melts.

Sawnie Morris

Frog Song

We've made two trips bearing groceries and books between the
car and the house in the leaf-splattered dark, before we
    sense it's not crickets — their adamant chirp, the rasping
        of shiny black   appendages   thickening fall air
          it's the balloon-lipped song of frog ululation, that
   frank mating cry, a synchronization, frenzied throb, sprung from
   hard-packed dirt. Frogs   among ant ziggurats & cactus
palms, frogs hidden below sage fronds freighted by moonlight.
Domed   galaxies of sound   *ribbiting* invisibly
      from the sum of an earth we have not yet fathomed. Their
     pulse fills our courtyard, ricochets against (and into)
   the shell of our house. Ecstatic swell springs from dogwood,
  plum, a rincon splashed with cinquefoil, the *latia* fence,
its stripped mountain aspen.   Frog song throngs
 from the roof, from *el otro lado* the house, as though that
pond we dream of each summer actually exists
    in our meadow-in-the-making, as though wheelbarrow
  tire ruts might — after three days faint rain — turn water-hollow
    ringed by mud-emeralds, among perse aster and wild
verde que te quiero verde   sedges.   But no — the
amphibian knot   was either never *in* our "back-
yard" — or has — at our footfall — dispersed — become a rush
        of shivering aural mirages, a density of
     unrestrained *i want i want* rippling into thick   night-
      blue distances, vivid in the cow dung lull, just *there* —
  it seems — and there — between scatter of earthen   buildings.
  Cloud leviathans glide in unison, cross mesa,
us, occluding the sky-eye. A few dogs bark.   One or
two windows are brushed into lit rectangles and the dirt
road turns damp path — we glimpse a hieroglyph of   tracks — mine —
  from long ago — this morning — when I was some other
      animal — in the dream world — where a frog stance intimates
   receptive attitudes and the oval   marriage hymn
turns upward thrust.   Out here, in the open   salvia-flats, frogs

are toads — their tense and release unfallow us. Thousands,
            in one-night clans. Miraculously strange (though it's
only normal), how they shake off their skin-cloaks, emerge
            from self-internment, let go strands of slimy globules
any place resembling echo. What astonishment —
they've been *with us* — all these years — in push-hands motion with
acrobatic weather. O Gaia, we've just been too
distracted — so sure we knew our relative
habitat. Come wet dream. Come sere metamorphosis.

Aimee Nezhukumatathil

Mr. Cass and the Crustaceans

Whales the color of milk have washed ashore
in Germany, their stomachs clogged full
of plastic and car parts. Imagine the splendor
of a creature as big as half a football field—

the magnificence of the largest brain
of any animal—modern or extinct. I have
been trying to locate my fourth grade
science teacher for years, Mr. Cass, who

gave us each a crawfish he found just past
the suburbs of Phoenix, before strip malls
licked every good desert with a cold blast
of Freon and glass. Mr. Cass, who played

soccer with us at recess, who let me check
on my wily, snappy crawfish in the plastic
blue pool before class started so I could place
my face to the surface of the water and see

if it still skittered alive. I hate to admit
how much this meant to me, the only brown girl
in the classroom. How I wish I could tell Mr. Cass
how I've never stopped checking the waters—

the ponds, the lakes, the sea. And I worry
that I've yet to see a sperm whale, except when
they beach themselves in coves. How many songs
must we hear from the sun-bleached bones

of a seabird or whale? If there were anyone on earth
who would know this, Mr. Cass, it's you—how even
bottle caps found inside a baby albatross corpse
can make a tiny ribcage whistle when the ocean wind

blows through it just right—I know wherever you are,
you'd weep if you heard this sad music. I think
how you first taught us kids to listen to water,
and I'm grateful for each story in its song.

Triggerfish Invective

The last time I sank my face in the neritic ocean
I found only beige and bleached out bones, not orange

and green coral fans. I spoke to angry underwater
ghosts in other languages I forgot I knew—full

of seaweed syllables and cracked shells.
Too many pale bodies march

their plastic fins over this coral, take selfies
on the coral, scrub coral clean of leafy food.

Not even leaving a scintilla of small-shelled
meats. The ghosts answer with a cackle and hiss

and light-scatter. The sea in this bay once curved
full of cucumbers and other funny vegetables, some

with fin and some with spine. Here the sea
like a swollen ring of motion burst—here the sea

throws a dozen fish with a pointed snout toward
me. I never thought I'd see triggerfish in real life

but here they are—almost a warning or last chance.
Why else would they activate their trigger fin

and hold on to coral bones with no more promise?
I am certain I will gain an anklet of tiny bites

from these humuhumunukunukuapua'a and why not:
for all the fish I see now, there were thousands

more just last year. And the last year. And the last.
The underwater ghosts only send out mondegreens.

Some scattered pale green light. A cackle and hiss.

January Gill O'Neil

The River Remembers

Here the water is silt-brown,
        stretches mile-wide,
                flat as a washed-out conveyor belt,
        an unhemmed rumble strip.
I can't read the River, can't see my hand
when it plunges elbow-deep
        to feel the cool against
                the Mississippi heat—
        hot as a dog's mouth.
Here we canoe for hours
through swirling eddies,
        watch the trash barges
                and towboats travel downstream.
        The River glistens hard as broken glass.
Here, everything is fluid.
In lower Mississippi, the South's south,
        where the two-lane blacktop cuts through
                an infinity of flat: cotton, soybean, corn.
        Farm, farm, tumbledown shack.
Creeks and rivers bifurcate the land like blood veins.
Here, the GPS gives up.
        New islands form at the current's whim
                and what is untouched grows lush and verdant.
        Willow and privet border the collapsing coastline.
A carp leaps into the boat when it hears us coming.
We stop here in an oxbow, gumbo mud sticks to our feet.
        River rock. Plastic. Fossils. Gar.
                Raccoon and coyote leave tracks in the rust-colored sand.
        The slaves—sold down the river—hid here,
waited for their chance to escape up north,
hid in caves, fled to the Twin Cities and Canada,
        their fate at the mercy of the river's next rise.
                Here's the nadir of our suffering,
        which started in one place to end in another.
Here's where flow and marvel and history converge.
This harmjoy. This beautiful sadness.

Cecily Parks

Girlhood

was when I slept in the woods
bareheaded beneath jagged
stars and the membranous
near-misses of bats, when
I tasted watercress,
wild carrot, and sorrel,
when I was known
by the lilac I hid beside,
and when that lilac, burdened
by my expectations of lilacs,
began a journey
without me, as when
the dirt road sang, *O,*
rugosa rose, farewell,
and ran behind the clipped
white pine hedge into
the immeasurable
heartbreaks of the field

Lynn Pattison

When even the north grew too hot

We move into the water. Most understand there is no point in bringing anything—the others learn quickly, belongings floating away, dissolving, freezing up or bogging them down. Simple needs rule. We share the work. Some gather kelp, crustaceans, duckweed. Others, the most tolerant of heat, go out to harvest succulents that have taken over the land. Dragon fruit and barrel cactus, low-growing sedum, and prickly pear. And aloe—most of us need it as our skin softens and peels underwater. We take readily to birthing in warm shallows. But swimming is slow business, we miss our cars and motorcycles. The inventive among us explore the adaptation of boats for towing us to the other shore. The young form spontaneous "schools" and travel through the river en masse. We don't know how to educate them for this life. Math, surely—but reading? As we learn the topography of our new world, we'll teach them to make maps in their heads. Athletes among us compete in among the rapids or test themselves against the current. We begin to learn the ancient language of the sturgeon, the whispers of minnows. The tailwhip and body-smack alarms of trout. Teenagers, watching the mating dances of turtles, take to fluttering their fingertips around the face of the beloved, chin-rubbing and face-stroking. The ones being wooed learn from the turtles as well and master clear ways to say "no." We are often content. We study the moon. Think about praying to her, thankful for cool nights. We could ask for change, make promises.

Andrew Payton

War Road

On the breeze is the mango rot of June; on the breeze are the bodies of hundreds of maggots tossed from the compost bucket to a nearby granite boulder, doubled over each other, falling to the ground and carried off by swarms of black ants; on the breeze is a vulture, scouting death; on the breeze is the voice of the river, pounding along the road below; on the breeze is the chatter of hens, the prehistoric whinny of the neighbor's burro, the hissing cicadas and the shrieking geckos; on the breeze is smoke from the woodstove, the leaves of the drought-choked límon, the purple petals of the wisteria, the breath of the forest heard in a thousand shivering palms; on the breeze is an armed jeep, its diesel cough and the laughter of its men and its burlap sacks of coca leaves, hewn, packaged, portaged, headed for unknown seaports; on the breeze is the paid silence of every neighbor, scratching through kitchens and courtyards and knotting empty hammocks; and on the breeze is the soil, scraped bare and mineral-rich—blood, volcano, gunpowder, and manure—burning every animal eye that asks, calling the gods by every name, please to make it rain.

Tommy Pico

from Nature Poem

The stars are dying

like always, and far away, like what you see looking up is a death knell
from light, right? Light

years. But also close, like the sea stars on the Pacific coast. Their little
arms lesion and knot and pull away

the insides spill into the ocean. Massive deaths. When I try to sleep I
think about orange cliffs, bare of orange stars. Knotted, glut. Waves are
clear. Anemones n shit. Sand crabs n shit. Fleas. There are seagulls
overhead. Ugh I swore to myself I would never write a nature poem.

The sand is fine. They say it's not Fukushima. I feel fine, in the sense
that I feel very thin—I been doin Tracy Anderson DVD workouts on
YouTube, keeping my arms fit and strong. She says *reach, like you are
being pulled apart*

I can't not spill. Sometimes it, sometimes . . . what you see is what you
glut. There are sometimes insides.

~

~

The world is infected

Systemic pesticides get absorbed by every cell of the plant, accumulate
in the soil, waterways

kiss the bees

knees, knees (in a Guns N' Roses way)

goodbye.

The world is a bumble bee

in the sense that, *who cares?*

My thumb isn't terribly green but it's terribly thumbing at me

it seems foolish to discuss nature w/out talking about endemic poverty

which seems foolish to discuss w/o talking about corporations given human agency which seems foolish to discuss w/o talking about colonialism which seems foolish to discuss w/o taking about misogyny

In the deepest oceans

the only light is fishes—

luciferin and luciferase mix ribbons flutter in the darkness

I am so dumb thinking about this makes me cry I am so dumb

~

~

The perigee moon haloes the white comforter in a Beyoncé way.

You shine like a bar of soap in the shadows.

The perigee moon is above both of us, in Portland, in NYC, in San Diego, in Hong Kong, Abu Dhabi, Guaynabo, Sri Lanka

Know the moon is inescapable tonight

and the tuft of yr chest against my shoulder blades—

This is the kind of nature I would write a poem about

~

~

You can't be an NDN person in today's world

and write a nature poem. I swore to myself I would never write a nature poem. Let's be clear, I hate nature—hate its *guts*

I say to my audience. There is something smaller I say to myself:

I don't hate nature at all. Places have thoughts—hills have backs that love being stroked by our eyes. The river gobbles down its tract as a metaphor but also abt its day. The bluffs purr when we put down blankets at the downturn of the sun and laugh at a couple on an obvi OkCupid date

and even more stellar, the jellybean moon sugars at me. She flies and beams and I breathe.

Fuck that. I recant. I slap myself.

Let's say I live in NYC. Let's say I was the first person in my family to graduate college. Let's say UGH I like watching *New Girl* on Hulu.

This is the difference:

Some see objects in the Earth, where I see lungs. Sky mother falls thru a hole, lands on a turtle.

Hole is my favorite band.

~

~

When a star dies, it becomes any number of things
like a black hole, or a documentary.

The early universe of our skin was remarkably smooth
now I stand in a rapidly dampening Christina Aguilera tee

The first stars were born of a gravity, my ancestors—
our sky is really the only thing same for me as it was for them,
which is a pretty stellar inheritance

I don't know how they made sense of that swell, how they survived
long enough to make me, and am sort of at war with sentimentality,
    generally

but that absence of an answer, yet suggestion of meaning
isn't ultimately that different from a poem
So I've started reading the stars

Nothing is possible until it happens, like digesting sulfur instead of
    sunlight
or friends with benefits

Poems were my scripture and the poets, my gods
but even gods I mean especially gods are subject to the artifice
of humanity.

I look up at the poem, all of them up there in the hot sky and fall
into the water, a stone

~

What if I really do feel connected to the land?

What if the mountains around the valley where I was born

What if I see them like faces when I close my eyes

What if I said hi to them in the mornings and now all their calls go to voicemail

What if I would ride my big wheels down the drive too fast headfirst into the chaparral and I'd steal myself from them scratchy having felt the pulse

What if I said sorry under my breath when I sat on moss on the rock at the crick behind myself

I would look like a freaking moron basket case

I get so disappointed by stupid NDNs writing their dumb nature poems like grow up faggots

I look this thought full in the face and want to throw myself into traffic

~

Admit it. This is the poem you wanted all along.

~

It's hard to be anything

but a pessimist

when you feel the Earth rotting away on so many home pages and Taylor Swift is an idiot and cigarettes cost an arm and a leg

I'm on a porch petting kitties and there is lavender in the air. The sun is over the hill and my friend Roy knows the names of all the plants in his front yard. One of the kitties is named Witch Baby and she likes to perch around your neck.

The air is clear, and all across Instagram—peeps are posting pics of the sunset.

Catherine Pierce

Anthropocene Pastoral

In the beginning, the ending was beautiful.
Early spring everywhere, the trees furred
pink and white, lawns the sharp green
that meant *new*. The sky so blue it looked
manufactured. Robins. We'd heard
the cherry blossoms wouldn't blossom
this year, but what was one epic blooming
when even the desert was an explosion
of verbena? When bobcats slinked through
primroses. When coyotes slept deep in orange
poppies. One New Year's Day we woke
to daffodils, wisteria, onion grass wafting
through the open windows. Near the end,
we were eyeletted. We were cottoned.
We were sundressed and barefoot. *At least
it's starting gentle*, we said. An absurd comfort,
we knew, a placebo. But we were built like that.
Built to say *at least*. Built to reach for the heat
of skin on skin even when we were already hot,
built to love the purpling desert in the twilight,
built to marvel over the pink bursting dogwoods,
to hold tight to every pleasure even as we
rocked together toward the graying, even as
we held each other, warmth to warmth,
and said sorry, *I'm sorry, I'm so sorry* while petals
sifted softly to the ground all around us.

Arlene Plevin

Tikkun Olam

Near the shores of Lake Washington
geese strut,
nibble the banks for food.
Water iris, delicate as infants' hands,
hold their bright yellow above the water.

There is a swirl of blackberry bramble,
avoidable thorns, bits of wrappers,
and the rotting protoplasm of memory
before world repair.

The Atlantic Ocean off
Long Beach, Long Island,
my father and his daughters
ages twelve and six and one
learning to float
in large salty waves
each of us our own raft.

Beyond Long Beach, beyond
the tempered waters of Lake Washington, beyond
the Atlantic,
Alan Kurdi, age three,
a Kurd from Syria,
clutches the shores of Italy.
Stones stipple his cheeks,
create egg-shaped bruises
like large thumbs pressed
in and on.

Both hands stretch
away from the Mediterranean Sea
as if his father might grasp
and drag him back.
His small bottom swaddled
and plump.

He exists between slumber
and waking,
waiting for love
to lift him into the arms
of his brother, his mother, his father.

Distance chokes our throats,
stuffs the path
between voice and heart.
His body folded in
upon itself,
washed up near a line of land,
the photo of

his smallness.

Vivian Faith Prescott

How to Yoik the Stikine River

Remove your shoes at the edge of our island. Close your eyes and fly your mind north to the headwaters—Mount Umbach, 6,000 feet above sea level to a chain of small lakes. Tilt your head back and let the first sounds take a meandering course. *Trust this process,* said your yoik teacher. Turn your mind west, then northwest, flow south along the Three Sisters Range, across highway, enter a deep canyon, cut through plateaus, and swiftly fall into a narrow channel. Squeeze yourself between walls of volcanic rock. Flow north past stratovolcanoes, and downstream to Telegraph Creek. Carry a riverboat in your mind filled with tourists and locals, float an old cottonwood log down past Cousin's Blue Bird floathouse, and a rickety moose camp. Meander past kids in their orange life jackets swimming off the dock at Twin Lakes. Flow-fly past the hot tub over two nude bathers, and past "The Desert" with the picnickers eating smoked salmon sandwiches on the sand. Drift near the cabins on Farm Island. Flow through the memories of Grandfather homesteading, my mother and her first home as a toddler watching moose eat the garden's carrots and watching stars streaking overhead across another river of sky. Catch a glint of salmon, hear the sea lion's bellow. Surge home, past the airport lights, past the old derelict boats rotting on the beach, past the harbors, and line of highway, to touch the rocky island shore. There, cold-kiss the current across your toes, suck up the notes into your legs, reach belly and breath. Draw the river in. Fill up with a sandbar, spin in a whirlpool. Open your mouth and make a sound like gravel. Scrape like a cottonwood tree sloughing off the riverbank into the slough. Sound like silt and grit. Become the Shtax'heen.

At a nearby glacier, I heard a yoik for a child

Dovdna *is a very simple joik that the child can easily recognize.*
— ELIN KÅVEN AND JUNGLE SVONNI

I was born from a river of ice
with ancestors clutching hands nearby.

I was born with eyes splashed
with the witness of distant stars.

Born as morning slipped
from night into the neighborhood,

as the doe leaped through the still silhouette
of the barn tree and ran down the dirt road.

Born to conjure glaciers into a traditional
Song with sound drawn on coastlines.

And here I am, new from mask of night,
somewhere between sunset and gray light,

where I've burrowed out from beneath
the dreams my ancestor women have chanted up

to inhabit this present shape, to inhabit
this rain-drenched day intoned with

silt-laden words, like wind over grass flats.

Jessica Purdy

After Watching Lior Patel's "Aerial Timelapse of Sheep
Herding" and Søren Solkær's "Amorphous Flocks of
Starlings Swell above the Danish Marshlands"

Released from their pens, the sheep
flow out like plasma and platelets
they pulse through valves of gates
into the veins of pathways, pooling
out past the path to pasture.
Each turn is a method of staying
together. Their white wool blurs
the lines around the individual
and makes it one whole liquid
body pushed by one heart. And think
of the starling murmurations
in autumn, how they swarm
and flow keeping each other warm
and whole. The one bird out-
numbered by the flock that eclipses it,
separates, snaps, undulates like the elastic
of kneaded bread dough. Swallowed
into the crowd which becomes
a made thing itself. Hypnotizing.
Enough to make a person forget
they're breathing air and not water—
to remember salmon swimming up-
river, whose reproductive
instinct is powerful enough
to scale waterfalls, only to die
after spawning in the place where
they were born; to think of the pads
of thumbs bumping over knots
in your trapezius, not just the way
it feels to you, but how the masseuse
must navigate the landscape

of musculature by touch, sliding over
a membrane of oil; to think how
the current returns with the tides
in a brackish estuary. How the fist
of your heart opens, constricts—conjures
the glide and lift of a goldfinch in flight.

Jane Satterfield

Emily Brontë's Advice for the Anthropocene

Hers is a Green and animal beyond.
— STEVIE DAVIES, *EMILY BRONTË: HERETIC*

          Haworth was a maze
of multiplying middens, mills, the pumped-up
clouds of industry, heathered moors a haven in
a century's shrinking space. Tempting, yes,
to stick to chores, scrub the parlour carpet,
remain, in fact, remote. But as the saying goes,
there is no later. This *is* later—arctic ice melts,
shears off; strange calvings stun the circumspect
to speech. If Emily were here today,
what would she say? Though twilight calls
for a generous pour, it's better to learn dark
sonatas, the heart's own haul of grief.
The soul's compass is—or ought to be—
set straight for the storm. Some species
die without a fellow creature's comfort—
sparrows sometimes fail to thrive when solitary.
The auk's line, I've read, unraveled when stumblers
dropped the eggs. Troubadours enshrine
the human truths—lies, betrayals, love
gone astray. What else would she tell us?
Aim to take dictation—a rabbit
grooming in the grass calls down the watchful hawk,
the robin's clutch in turn attracts the foraging crow.
And would we listen to her counsel
as we stand stoic in the bracing air, embrace
the static stare of endlings? *Look up,* she'd say,
you will come to call them kin.

Rebecca Seiferle

In the unending rain

night leopards of the grass
pour out into the night,

a river pulse,
a flowing stream

across drenched ground, their tiny antlers
slowly turning

to some leaf, the silver keeling
shining beneath their dappled backs

and who will sing their
hermaphroditic beauty,

their patient, singular,
forms,

though, perhaps, they already
sing themselves

at ultrasonic frequencies
the human ear can't hear

*

the dreams were so real—turning a mountain curve
into a deluge, the highway disappearing between the surging waves
that, years later, I thought it had really happened, that flood
a memory of my family just escaping,
my fear of who to save—

but my mother laughed and said *that never happened,
it was just a dream, a foolish
vision*

*

yet now I could be looking at that dream, embodied,
detached in this photograph in Kansas somewhere,
where some man has gotten out of his car and stands looking ahead
to depths where, ordinarily,
his way home would be, a road
that is now made of water,
a lake extending in all directions

*

the whole world's underwater, our kitchen fills with slow brown swamp,
    and even along
the Seine, the Louvre is shuttered as they struggle to carry to safety
a painted smile, a marble gesture, some penciled pentimento

*

where's higher ground,
what's human floating here forever,
our fingers turning prune-like, grasping
a floating chair becomes a flotation device,
while sludge surges to first-floor ceilings,

it goes on for hours, has gone on for how long clinging,
clung, we cannot remember land or grass beneath our feet, unending
ending is upon us, and we reminiscence of how once, briefly, we imagined
the span of one eternal day
but even the raven is not returning

*

I try to reassure myself that life persists,
some species, perhaps
these leopard slugs,
will outlast us,
Limax maximus,

with its homing
instincts and its ability for associative learning
its composite of the imagined
and the silver iridescent track
its leaving leaves upon the leaf

the *Limacidae* family,
the *Gastropoda* class, the phylum of *Mollusca*,
of the *Animalia* kingdom,
among the largest of keeled slugs,
air breathing, terrestrial,

but wearing an oblong shield that expands
when it's irritated, a calcitic shell, internal
but attached and visible under the skin, making an angle
of 80 degrees when moving, beneath
the mantle marbled with black,

moving like the keel of a boat

sailing through the flooded grass

as all we know
are rising waters
where all the cities we have loved

now drown

Alafia Nicole Sessions

Love Poem as Omnipastoral

for and after Ariana, Vievee, and my sister, Cecilia

Step into the stall of my heart, where it is safe.
Where you can see the pasture, prepare for its

magic and malice. Yes it rains here, but I have prayed
and I've known thirst. Together, we'll collect the skygift

with barrels when we can, with hands and mouths
when we must. Yes it sometimes floods, but how else

do you learn what sleeps beneath the topsoil, how do
you expose those willing to eat the dead, find the shaman?

It's true I only know you through papyrus, lyric. But isn't it love
between women, both wet and woven, that has saved us?

Did you know the distance between two glades is laughter—
even when one is ablaze. Beloved, you are scared

the ghosts that rise from the compost will envy our joy,
snatch the pleasure we braised from their bones, their loss

still audible in the meadow. We'll never know how much
a branch can hold under a body's weight, or so we pray.

You're afraid we will stop turning, that our roots will rot,
but I know you like I know our garden, which rows rely

on the breath of the sun, which of your tender leaves
require shade. Listen. I will chiffonade my body for you,

curl the ripples of my thighs into Scotch bonnet sauce,
cut the heat with my cooled tears. Sweeten your bloodline

with weedsong, sound my drum between you and the wolf.
Once, we dreamed a purple earth in which your eyes turned

violet, the season to return you to the soil. In the now season,
chrysalis son asks, grappling to understand scale, *are there*

100 billion ants for every person on the planet? Daughter, quiet as silt, studies the coyote's crawl but cannot comprehend war.

On our backs, tracking honeydew moon, we are all marvel, crippled by the expanse, the speckled quilt through which

the egun flew. You tell me you will feed my seed from your own body, the field, should I ascend early, should I bolt. You'll teach

the hungry how to hold the chicken neck before the spin. Which animals are predator, which are kin. How to respect both.

You'll teach him how to plant, chop, and drop alfalfa. Her how to nourish the land, when the sky is blank, the moon new, with her

blood. When my organs cue the nocturne you will bury the carbon of my body, bare, bone kissing clay. You will let the hurricane roll

from your eyes as I become mycelium. I'll conjure my infinite hands, push up a single fruiting body, and I will feed you, again.

Leona Sevick

Fallout

Following the light, their golden
faces are, by sundown, heavy
and low with cares. Still, I can't tear

myself away, not now. You'd say
do it, run from this bright hot porch,
this lovely field of sunflowers

mocking you with their likeness,
with their sacrifice. Mornings
they are young and fresh, their tiny

florets dripping dew while threaded
roots finger delta soil, seeking
copper and zinc, drawing them

up and into leaves and stalks.
They hold it all—mouths cupping
poisons unseen by the casual

observer. In Fukushima, scientists
planted fields of them, delighting
villagers until others came and cut

them down, toted away polluted
carcasses. You'd say I can't be
someone else's medicine.

Watch me.

Samyak Shertok

The Last Beekeeper

Let it be said Ama was the last
Himalayan beekeeper.
When she harvested honey barehanded
in the stone house we lived in, she took not juniper
smoke but song to the hive.
A home is one flower
and a thousand stings.
The bees flew into her oiled black hair
and when she combed it, down
fell rhododendrons.
Let it be said not a single bee
stung her. The summer before I left
home, she fed me raw
honey from her palm every night.
In the dark I learned to hold
bees in my throat, one
for every ancestor. Let it be said
not a single bee died.
                      Now
every time I misremember the word
of the Horse-Ghost, I get stung
in my windpipe. With each perished
bee, Ama becomes
more smoke. Let it be said
if you plunge your hand into an abandoned hive
you will still get stung. At night
Ama plucks stingers from my tongue
with her nails. Each barb she binds
with her lock, and her crown
grows more thorn than rhododendron.
This way, Moonbug, you will recognize me
when I return. I've waited
with one thousand dead
bees in my mouth to say your name
let it be said.

A Brief History of Hunger

The sky snakeroot smoke and rasping—a terrible light swallowed up
the village. Up close: monsters of dirt, without number. Their wings
sickled and shining: fairies rapacious, red red. They sheathed the
cedars and barley fields ash yellow. Soon we could see neither land
nor sky. We bolted the windows: the Teeth of the Wind kept us quiet
in the dark. At dawn we discovered they couldn't open their wings
soon enough. The village was unleashed upon them. In the burlap
sacks, reed baskets, gagris, woolen hats, and shawls we gathered the
unblessed harvest like fallen leaves. We poured them into the boiling
pots, plucked their devil heads—their faces so like our amas'—and
wings and legs into a pile of dinner for the cats and dogs and crows,
fried what remained in burnt ghee until they crunched between our
teeth. We ate them, each one now the size of a girl's finger, dipped in
wild honey. Some even smoked them in bamboo skewers for winter.
Where did they come from? Where were they going? They knew only
hunger. They ravaged the leaves as though they had to pass through
all the green on the land to get to the other side. But we, too, knew
hunger. If we waited for the gods, come winter we would be hurling
our lambs and newborns into the same ravine. So we spared no leaf,
no blade, no sky, no angel. Akhes prophesied they'd return in twelve
years, but we never saw them again. That summer we turned famine
into feast. For nine days we ate nothing but what had come to eat us.
That hunger lives in our blood now and our children's and their
children's, and it will not stop until the last green is cut.

John Shoptaw

Pangolin Scales

You
wrote, Miss
Moore, about how
the pangolin, streaming
at high night from its stone-
lipped burrow, trespassing on Belgian
Congo moonlight, gibbous as a bell curve
from its paginated tail down to its
gummed tongue, prolonged
for trickling down ant-
slickened trunk
crevices,
would

swirl
headlong down
the impenetrable drain it
makes of itself (Malay *pengguling*:
up-rolling thing), an involute, inexplicable
globe, plate lapping overlapping scalloped plate.
Only now, Miss Moore, I hate to report, it's plucked
like a junglesop fruit with its prehensile stem,
and handed off to traffickers, who parade it
into some high-rolling private dining
room in Guangdong or in Ho
Chi Minh City where its
throat's
scis-

sored
steaming at the
upscale table as ardent
proof of freshness and gratitude to
the client whose *ummm!* stimulates the ritual

consummation of the handshake deal. *Considered
a delicacy*, an anthropologically delicate phrase you'd
have relished, Miss Moore. But why? *Nostalgie
de la boue?* Or a nostalgia to be bushmeat
eaters minus the mud in the wild west
of Southeast China, where
businessmen mean
business?

From
the black tricorner
of my notebook ajar, these
armored stanzas gleam expectantly.
Yes, Miss Moore, there's more. Olive, tan, and
golden brown toenail scales, skinned or worked off
living pangolins one by one like artichoke leaves, scales
soft at first and milk white on the besotted nursling
riding its mammal's tail like a bath toy, ton
upon ton from Malaysia, Indonesia,
Zimbabwe, in luggage, under
timber, red bean sacks,
bound

for West
Berkeley Wellness, say,
in the mild West of the East Bay
on 7th Street, away from traffic, where
maternal practitioners of Traditional Chinese
Medicine, codified by Chairman Mao in the 1950s,
invite us over from their homepage window,
while visitors positively Yelp, and (now
unsearchable) pangolin scales, cool
and salty as the Pacific, are
administered to promote
menstrual flow and
lactation.

Martha Silano

Self-Portrait as Southern Resident Orca

For everybody *I'm speechless! Damn it, I gotta go get my camera!*
For *this must be the happiest pod.*
For you can hear them saying *There she goes again. Big one! Wow!*
For you can hear them clapping, laughing.
For I swim through the research proving there is no difference in the
    lifespan of being born at Sea World or in the wild.
For 700,000 years of genetic distinction, 700,000 years of a distinct
    dialect evolving.
For I was misnamed *whale killer* by Spanish explorers.
For I am a dolphin.
For each year I ingest 7 million quarts of motor oil washing into the
    Salish Sea.
For despite being banned in 1979, each day I push through 1.5 billion
    pounds of PCBs.
For in my fat stores I carry your coal mining, electric appliance
    dependence, insecticides.
For because of you I brush against carcinogenic furans.
For I am a mother carrying her dead newborn. For I have been carrying
    him for days.
For thanks to my contaminated milk, he is even more toxic than I.
For you might call this behavior a tour of grief, but I have been driving
    my baby to the surface so he can take a breath.
For my solitude grows scarce.
For your ships interfere with my clicks, whistles, and pulses, with
    knowing where the salmon are—species, speed, size.
For the sea and I are both wide.
For the water I glide through is poisoned with viscosity index improvers;
    for the lapping is laced with alkaline additives and sealants; for if you
    read more closely, search more carefully, you will learn PCBs were not
    banned but permitted in smaller concentrations.
For I can certainly experience intense emotion.
For Monsanto's CEO makes 19 million a year but the Chemical Action Plan
    lacks funding; for there is no government strong enough to save me.

For behold my spy-hopping!
For who can resist my one-syllabled, Darth Vader–like exhale?
For google *biomagnification*.
For the dusty road is my demise.
For the highway's yellow line, I die.
For I'm corralled not by my mistakes but yours.
For the doors of my duration are closing.

Dorsía Smith Silva

Hurricane María Countdown

10

The neighbors have gone hunting
for sheets of wood at Home Depot
and water at Walmart.

9

We tape plastic over the windows
and then snap the silver tormenteras
into place: clang, bang, clang.

8

Las noticias on the television recites
the warning: María is coming.
But it wasn't supposed to be this
bad: a whirlwind Category 5.

7

The beach is getting half-eaten. The
seashells drowning in new graves.

6

I do not see a single bird. I grieve.

5

The neighborhood school's windows
and roof get swallowed by a rushing
torrent.

4

Some satos make their way through
the liquid bombs and dash under a
car.

3
Emergency lights flood the airport.
They engulf whatever good humor
was left.

2
Billboards by Plaza las Américas
rock back and forth like line laundry
before hitting the ground.

1
There is something grinding outside
with a loud rasp. I can barely hear las
noticias' wail about María.

0
The last stench before the power
crawls away.

I pause to give gratitude to green

green that breathes across sky's steel birdcage
green after what hurricane season can muster
it gives me a sign of hope like garden's scented
staircase collecting sunlight whenever I come
closer to the teeth of desperation every evening
sitting in the tunnels of gray violence cars rotating
to spiraled highways green messages remember me
here here here green glows like a future life's
invitation I call out like my mother in the doorway
won't you stay for supper take a place right next to me

Jake Skeets

In the Fields

with lines from D. A. Powell

We unyoke owl pellets from marrow
in desert meadow. His mouth pigeon eye

a torch, womb turned flower. He, still a boy,
dug from cactus skull. Undress into bark

beetles. He unlearns how to hold a fist
with my hand. Bursts into dandelion

seeds. *We are all beautiful at least once.*
Mud water puddles along enamel.

Eyeteeth blossom into osprey. Our bones
dampen like snowmelt under squirrel grass.

We could be boys together finally
as milk vetch, tumbleweed, and sticker bush.

We can be beautiful again beneath
the sumac, yarrow, and bitter water.

Anthropocene: A Dictionary

definitions from the Navajo–English Dictionary, *by Leon Wall and William Morgan*

dibé bighan: sheep corral

juniper beams caught charcoal in the late summer morning
night still pooled in hoofprints; deer panicked run from water

ooljéé' bináʼadinídíín: moonlight

perched above the town drowned in orange and streetlamp
the road back home dips with the earth

                            shines black in the sirens

bit'a' : its sails or—its wing(s)

        driving through the mountain pass
                dólii, mountain bluebird, swings out—
        from swollen branches
I never see those anymore, someone says

diyóół   : wind (

                wind (more of it) more wind as in (to come up)
                plastic bags driftwood the fence line

nihootsoii

          :   evening—somewhere northward fire
                        twists around the shrublands;
                sky dipped in smoke—twilight

     —there is a word for this,

                        someone says

           :   deidííłid, *they burned it*

           :   kódeiilyaa, *we did this*

Danez Smith

dear white america

i've left Earth in search of darker planets, a solar system revolving too near a black hole. i've left in search of a new God. i do not trust the God you have given us. my grandmother's hallelujah is only outdone by the fear she nurses every time the blood-fat summer swallows another child who used to sing in the choir. take your God back. though his songs are beautiful, his miracles are inconsistent. i want the fate of Lazarus for Renisha, want Chucky, Bo, Meech, Trayvon, Sean & Jonylah risen three days after their entombing, their ghost re-gifted flesh & blood, their flesh & blood re-gifted their children. i've left Earth, i am equal parts sick of your go back to Africa & i just don't see race. neither did the poplar tree. we did not build your boats (though we did leave a trail of kin to guide us home). we did not build your prisons (though we did & we fill them too). we did not ask to be part of your America (though are we not America? Her joints brittle & dragging a ripped gown through Oakland?). i can't stand your ground. i'm sick of calling your recklessness the law. each night, i count my brothers. & in the morning, when some do not survive to be counted, i count the holes they leave. i reach for black folks & touch only air. your master magic trick, America. now he's breathing, now he don't. abra-cadaver. white bread voodoo. sorcery you claim not to practice, hand my cousin a pistol to do your work. i tried, white people. i tried to love you, but you spent my brother's funeral making plans for brunch, talking too loud next to his bones. you took one look at the river, plump with the body of boy after girl after sweet boi & ask why does it always have to be about race? because you made it that way! because you put an asterisk on my sister's gorgeous face! Call her pretty (for a black girl)! because black girls go missing without so much as a whisper of where?! because there are no amber alerts for amber-skinned girls! because Jordan boomed. because Emmett whistled. because Huey P. spoke. because Martin preached. because black boys can always be too loud to live. because it's taken my papa's & my grandma's time, my father's time, my mother's time, my aunt's time, my uncle's time, my brother's & my sister's time . . . how much time do you want for your progress? i've left Earth to find a place where my kin can be safe, where black people ain't but people the same color as the good, wet earth, until that means something, until then i bid you well, i bid you war, i bid you our lives to gamble with no more. i've left Earth & i am touching everything you beg your telescopes to show you. i'm giving the stars their right names. & this life, this new story & history you cannot steal or sell or cast overboard or hang or beat or drown or own or redline or shackle or silence or cheat or choke or cover up or jail or shoot or jail or shoot or jail or shoot or ruin

this, if only this one, is ours.

dream where every black person is standing by the ocean

& we say to her
>	*what have you done with our kin you swallowed?*

& she says
>	*that was ages ago, you've drunk them by now*

& we don't understand

& then one woman, skin dark as all of us
>	walks to the water's lip, shouts *Emmett*, spits

&, surely, a boy begins
>	crawling his way to shore

Tracy K. Smith

An Old Story

We were made to understand it would be
Terrible. Every small want, every niggling urge,
Every hate swollen to a kind of epic wind.

Livid, the land, and ravaged, like a rageful
Dream. The worst in us having taken over
And broken the rest utterly down.

                                   A long age
Passed. When at last we knew how little
Would survive us—how little we had mended

Or built that was not now lost—something
Large and old awoke. And then our singing
Brought on a different manner of weather.

Then animals long believed gone crept down
From trees. We took new stock of one another.
We wept to be reminded of such color.

Heidi Staples

Prayer

Bower for air in heaving, nomadic

Leap fly ray. Pry fling sum flume. spry fill breeze sun,

Under's birth as lit is wind's heaving. soar live lush

Err's wets, has breeze

Mere fin throes blue fold wet is again's lush. sand rave lush is dei

Air day leap wet, finned

Roil rave lush dark stressed mass,

Lush breeze bower fin throes blue

Is splash a gleam's lush. spanned the

Noon off the far there, sand the sun. An and.

Page Starzinger

Galaxy Filament

Of time evaporating, of my mother's finger
running down my nose during the uncording
ceremony, after she died, the vast sky,
the Milky Way neighborhood,
and me, and David, and the black cat growing tumors,
rain falling, drops left over, puddles gathering,
reflecting the baby birds, black millipedes dropping
off branches, white blossoms floating below cedar,
sunrays bleaching shells, stop signs fading,
a family of wild donkeys milling around
an outdoor basketball court at noon in high heat,
sargassum mats drifting from the horse latitudes
into Drunk Bay, flush with plastic waste and
eel nests, washing onto sandstone rocks,
a lost rubber raft cast ashore with a long towline dragging in the surf,
chickens jump-flapping off trash heaps filled with twisted stair railings
and corrugated roofs blown off by 30 tornados
of two Cat 5 hurricanes, red dust from the Sahara Desert
sifting toward us, nutrients feeding the phytoplankton
but also pathogenic bacteria of the genus *Vibrio*,
iguanas digging nests into the ground and burying their eggs
until hatchlings crack the shells, wait underground
until each emerges, then one after the other, in a line,
scratch their way out. A lone heron soars across the bay.

Rose Strode

Saint Cuthbert Proclaims the First Sanctuary for Birds, 676 A.D.

Maybe he recalled the night he stood in the sea to pray. The sun rose
over the bronze-pink ocean, a red host glowing,
and he glowed back with a strange euphoria brought on by extreme
cold. He'd intended to mortify his flesh but found
joy instead. They say a pair of otters played upon the beach, wrestling
and rubbing against each other, and when they saw his feet
they rubbed them too, curious to discover
what he might be, entrusting
themselves to him. In the lee of every stone
a crust of snow remained.

The multitudes of nesting eiders learned his gentle presence
kept predators away, so raised their young
along the stony paths where he walked daily, going slowly,
stopping often. He saw ducklings hatch
or fail to hatch, witnessed tenderness between the mated pairs,
the way they protected hatchlings not their own.
They perched beside him on the stone and seemed
content, yet knew when it was time to fly away. Like them, he knew
his time was near. He saw the way snow melts
even in the sheltered places. Maybe he wondered about the nature
of paradise.

Marcela Sulak

Lantana

Sorry about the haunting; I miss it, though, home. So I'm sniffing heat-split tomatoes, their splashed seeds, their earth, and the great ships of squash I'm loading onto the bike basket, plus there's a daughter who won't weed. Sometimes I think the haunt who laughed at my believed-ins palming the closet light and leering was once a man.

The wind breathing into my adolescence, the moonlight, might have been poison the crop dusters dropped; I caught it in my hat, my orange polyurethane flag over my head, my father's matching flag in step with mine across the field, marking the path for Marion flying overhead dropping clear crystals. Hard rain between NASA and the Bay City Nuclear Power Plant where we lived in the puddle pirated by Laffite, the Gulf of Mexico. Cancer coming for everyone. But our haunting wasn't that dread of the day I'll hear the brother with six, for example, children; too, I think my daughter old now enough to remember me in case. Friends say my life, it is blessed, not everything wanted, but who knows what drudgery, war, murder, or casualties of petty jealousies managed to escape me completely unaware and which ones this little act right now implicates or extricates

—I spend several days a week on this because if you let things go, the weeds take over in the garden. Though in Tel Aviv Eitan says, *Relax, we aren't farmers, we're weekend gardeners.* I'm coached on how to control systems I had no idea existed but trust their symptoms. I used to be more lonely and ecstatic, bound as I am these nights to home so that the midnight sea doesn't exist anymore for me, nor the stars so thick they used to press me into bed, rewire my head before I had a girl of my own.

That's lantana, I say walking my girl past their tiny paper plates of various colored flowerlets gathered into a single stem. I know that scent, the smell of sweat and of tomato vines. *No it's not poisoned we have it at home* I say meaning Texas.

Heather Swan

After

    There among the silences
find the ghost tree—

    the split black branches making
fissures in the clearing.

    Watch as the fog dresses
and undresses the wounds,

    the suppuration of bark,
so raw underneath.

    The birds can find
no purchase.

    Scavenge the esker,
make a circle of stones,

    kneel down wreathed in
feather and bracken.

    Prepare to knit yourself
back into the world.

Tess Taylor

from California Suites

[I. RAINY SEASON]

Season of mud, of swollen gullies,
storms lashing off the Pacific, flinging
wet across our solstice months.
We call this bitter damp the winter
but it is different than rosy cheeks or blizzards
or catalogs of kids in reindeer sweaters:
Our winter turns the hillsides emerald.
Suburbs reveal thoughtless paving; drains
gargle now where salmon spawned.
Plum blossoms eddy
next to candy wrappers.
Between storms, the light is mercury.
Huge wet sets hillsides careening,
hurtling down what fault line just thrust up.
Now ferns glisten, redwoods blacken.
Now cold buckeye seed & lemons come.
In rain, streets grow riverine,
ferrying our cargo to the ocean.
O cold spray & green reclaiming:
In you, we are all tributaries.

[IV. ESCROW]

In every sale, a list of ways
your home could be destroyed.
Flood, earthquake, fire.
Your house may end in mudslide,
be damaged by a rain of golf balls;
you may live downwind of poison breezes
off oil fields, refineries, or croplands.
You must assert you have
considered agricultural toxins; the risk

inherent in tectonic plates.
Signing on the dotted line allots you
a postcard plot of Golden State. Will
it be cancerous? God-willing
not to you. Your new house is younger
than your mother.
At your bottlebrush,
native hummingbirds.
Behind them, two huge redwoods wait.
In redwood years, these trees
are babies. They overlook
your fragile real estate.

Brian Teare

from Toxics Release Inventory

& / & / **&** / & / **&**

              endlessly :: see :: through this air,
     this ocean, this earth,

                   all matter quick, burst-
        ing into birth :: how high life
                     may go! how wide! how

deep extend below!
        writes Pope, & I hear instead
     of his praise the change

                we bring to the terms
        of life, how we make matter
               an antagonist

when industry goes
        so wide, so deep, & touches
     us so totally

                we find our final
        privacies violated ::
                  benzene & styrene,

toluene & n-
        hexane, carbon disulfide
     & acetone :: six

                toxics present in
        ninety-four to one hundred
                 percent of people

tested, both urban
        & rural, people whose blood
     & urine carries

                          the cost of merely
              breathing as they go to work ::
                                    & are not broken

by contaminants,
              or are not yet broken by
          the slow violence

                            latent in the wake
              of bioaccumulants
                              & synergistic

toxins stored in fat,
              in the liver & kidneys
          where one errancy

                          can birth an illness
              that quickens matter the way
                          the refinery

visits affliction
              upon working-class neighbors
          through onsite toxics

                          released into air ::
              breathing sulfuric acid
                          fumes leads to asthma

the way benzene gas
              fosters cognitive problems
          & leukemia

                          in extreme cases ::
              it's so bad, having these fumes
                          in your mouth, & not

knowing what they are,
              says activist Teresa
          Hill, who lives nearby.

                          with her kids who can't
              breathe without medical bills
                          totaling thousands ::

I write down *asthma*
                    cluster, environmental
           racism, under-

                                        line her words, then
                        a line of Merleau-Ponty's ::
                                        where are we to put

the limit between
                    the body & the world, since
           all the world is flesh? ::

                                        the question's stakes change
                        when I think of tasting fumes
                                        as I mouth the words ::

some marry the world
                    I write next in the notebook
           & I don't know what

                                        I mean by *marry*
                        or *world* :: what is the feeling
                                        that sends me walking

out of my childhood
                    into the pines behind it
           until grass rises

                                        above my head, field
                        a world more of things than facts,
                                        & sunset touches

the ceiling of seeds
                    I hide under :: what is it
           I feel as I walk

                                        back to the tight knot
                        each night ties around the house ::
                                        let the image be

my answer, I write,
                    let the image answer me ::
           when I clear the pines

I stand just outside
the scant light the house casts off ::
its steady edge *is*

the limit between
my body's flesh & the world's ::
the limit is learned

& gender teaches
us where to put it if race
doesn't :: white queer boy,

I marry the world
because, as a child pressing
against it, I feel

no limits to flesh,
just the crush of pine needles
& sticky resin,

the white commonplace
of feeling safe I seek out
when safety fails me

inside :: even then
I can accept the violence
that arises from

being a mammal,
our bloody given bodies
of glands & hormones,

our lust & fucking,
the ways we change as we age
& die :: but I hate

what happens inside
the house, the hierarchies
& made fake limits

of family life
enforced by Christ & paddle,
the petty moral

legalese peddled
       by people who try to shame
    my love for the flesh

              of the world whose flesh
      I share :: that is why I walk
              out of everywhere ::

Orchid Tierney

from a field guide to future flora

[COTTONWOOD OR MICROFLEECE]

cottonwood or microfleece trip the light fantastic with fairy hairs
    doctorbees apply salve   disinfect hives   oily butter
   something to sooth   fluff plumage like   fail helicopters
or furry teeth   drift in the wind   lose shapes in the skim
  of hungry grass   a desire for sexual motion conflicts
     with a lust to vegetate   catholic wish for stable employment in the air
to unionise for growth   an error in division   a salary of sunlight
        to migrate for new wages   whatever the forest can afford
it's amazing how sunlight returns the next day
    economic downdrafts rush kin to enraged whims of an angry grove
     to hues of rye   and bailey   that compete with rooty engines for talking
apiarian collusions   is a viscous charm   slimes in the bottom of thinking
   capitalism on the rock is a poor boss   a heat machine
partial dying   for a golden apple   umbilical cords   sprouting sheep
and pages of a book   sugar in the dirt   profitable extraction
   when all kin wants   a thriving wage of water   some nutrients

[FLOWERS ARE SLOW-MOVING COWS OF THE GLEBE]

      flowers are slow-moving cows of the glebe   and gentle observers
always facing the south   the light within kin's basin is brisk and sweet
     pleasant   the motion of day to night and all between
    is a negligible sensation   what matters is the eating
and communing of roots   small dramas are the exchanges of nutrients
   and bacteria   who pass knowledge like carnal letters
some flowers archive some forgotten pain in the stem down to the root
     hurt brings pleasure without joy
others tingle as a browning leaf   recalls a thickened past
without the radiance of language   there is a shared nod
between flowers   that history is absurd
              the temperature of grief is proof
      such matters the bacteria share like love letters

Alison Townsend

Northern Red Oak: Mercy

Lightning unzipped her once, blazing down her bark
soaked black with rain. It tore into her, just like that,

blasting her open to the shock of light with its burning
touch, the way a boy once entered me. A tree's sapwood

explodes when struck by a bolt, no choice but to stand still,
while the charge travels to earth, electricity absorbed in ways

I do not understand. I lay still, too, when it happened to me,
like a girl in a folk tale, stunned by what I had no name for.

Everything was quiet afterward. The rain pelted down
on the tree and me, all our secrets showing, her reddish bark

peeled back by fire, my flowered panties torn. The scar left
by it remains on the tree, neat black seam where her bark

inched slowly together, closing over the shredded pink wood,
like a body shutting a door. The strike might have broken her,

as it broke me for a time. But the oak didn't die, her sap scalded
within. She held on, standing tall at the bottom of the hill, roots

anchoring her to this place. I stayed upright, too, my scar
invisible, the psyche's gut stitches cinched tight within. An oak

tree isn't a woman. I am not an oak. I hesitate to braid our stories
together, not wanting to impose mine on hers. But what I love

most about the tree's wound is the place where she could not
seal herself completely shut. The wood there is white and smooth

as satin, the black slit splitting, fan-shaped, alluvial, down her trunk
to the plush delta of moss at her roots. It teaches me something,

broken beauty from which she regrew, in this oak savanna—
vanishing ecosystem we slowly "restore"—where trees talk

to one another through their roots and I sit at her base, the cool,
blue hands of rain watering our lives in ways I never imagined.

Natasha Trethewey

Elegy [I think by now the river must be thick]

for my father

I think by now the river must be thick
  with salmon. Late August, I imagine it

as it was that morning: drizzle needling
  the surface, mist at the banks like a net

settling around us—everything damp
  and shining. That morning, awkward

and heavy in our hip waders, we stalked
  into the current and found our places—

you upstream a few yards and out
  far deeper. You must remember how

the river seeped in over your boots
  and you grew heavier with that defeat.

All day I kept turning to watch you, how
  first you mimed our guide's casting

then cast your invisible line, slicing the sky
  between us; and later, rod in hand, how

you tried—again and again—to find
  that perfect arc, flight of an insect

skimming the river's surface. Perhaps
  you recall I cast my line and reeled in

two small trout we could not keep.
  Because I had to release them, I confess,

I thought about the past—working
  the hooks loose, the fish writhing

in my hands, each one slipping away
  before I could let go. I can tell you now

that I tried to take it all in, record it
    for an elegy I'd write—one day—

when the time came. Your daughter,
    I was that ruthless. What does it matter

if I tell you I *learned* to be? You kept casting
    your line, and when it did not come back

empty, it was tangled with mine. Some nights,
    dreaming, I step again into the small boat

that carried us out and watch the bank receding—
    my back to where I know we are headed.

Brian Turner

The Immortals

Bell-shaped and translucent, jellyfish begin their ascent from the ocean floor.
They've completed a novel process in the animal kingdom: transdifferentiation.
It's a reversal of the biological cycle as we know it—undoing the narrative arc
tracing birth to adulthood before the inevitable decline and death. The jellyfish
upend everything we know about death in flora and fauna. At the cellular level,
they grow *younger* when the time comes to die. They transform backward
into a nascent version of themselves before starting the process over.

It doesn't mean they are incapable of dying—it's simply not in their nature.
They rise through the midnight-dark waters and into bands of sunlight
the way thought forms in the subconscious before burning in waves
across the neocortex of the human brain. And as they rise,
fathom by fathom, they become lighter. As each incarnation
returns, history unfolds and the world is made new. They rise
into the Age of Agriculture with its domestication of wild grain,
with the comprehension of seed to stem to fruit. They witness
the emergence of cities. Wheels and alphabets and metallurgy.
Buddha and Confucius, Jesus and Mohammed. The Age of Flight
and the Age of Information. The jellyfish descend to regenerate
and then rise through it all, limpid and curious, as astronauts
step upon the lunar surface and as armies kill each other
without cease. Humans turn their thoughts toward Mars
and beyond, as the jellyfish sink down into the ancient shadow
where they have always gone, as if death were a form of sleep,
a dream from which they are revived, one lifetime to another,
cycling through the stages of life as the elastic architecture
of their bodies is made strange and new all at once. *Blooming.*

Starfields glimmer in the wavetops above. Sunlight scatters at dawn
and dusk. The ocean is a silver film of moonlight stilling itself.
And through it all, the jellyfish. The immortals. They have come
to watch galaxies loosen their spiraling stars as photons
shimmer on the interstellar breeze. They are steeped in time.
They have learned to reinvent themselves in defiance

of the body's undoing. They rise from their own deaths.
They rise from the bottom of the sea. Soft bells,
diaphanous and fine, the universe offers them wonder
and they gather in their multitudes to take it all in.

One Last Moment in the Vast City of Ants

With subterranean housing for millions, it's an abandoned city now,
left vacant. Imagine the labor it took to tunnel through, to carve out
each massive vault and to press forward, toiling without cease,
undaunted by the unyielding earth, resolute in the task, ants
tunneling passageways from one season to the next, each
with a lifespan of sixty days, at best, and still they pressed on,
generation by generation digging further into the sediment,
their claws and mandibles dismantling the hours set before them,
each destined to perish without seeing the vision to its end,
each glimpsing, perhaps, a sweeping monument of architecture
that later rendered scientists speechless by the scale of it.
Sunrise to sunset. Civilization by civilization.

When the city was alive with ants, the rains brought deluge,
storm-driven panic. Those on the surface were pummeled
by raindrops as large as the ants themselves, the water falling
through the empty sky from 2,500 feet above. Weak and strong alike
were carried away by floods, never to be seen by the colony again.
Those in the tunnels faced a torrent of water funneling down
with no end in sight, the roar of water and gravity their doom.

When scientists discovered this combed structure at their feet,
they poured several tons of concrete into vents and entryways—
flooding the passages and chambers below. Anything dead or alive
instantly entombed in liquid stone. Crews then removed the soil
in an area covering roughly five hundred square meters, eight meters
deep. They struggled to comprehend the planning, the logistics,
the social organization necessary to see it done.

In Brazil, where the excavated city lies open to the air, I imagine
one solitary ant pausing near the trees where the horizon-line
meets the sky. A small river of ants passes by, steadfast
in their labor and intention. And that lone ant, as curious a creature
as I am, looks back along the path as it chews a fibrous green leaf,
angling its anvil-shaped head now and then to consider the wind
swaying blades of grass in the valley below. Like some whisper
of the past. Some echo from long ago. Some old story about a city
lost in the earth, where the ancestors once rose in their multitudes
to take flight, a calamity in their wake which no one can remember
pushing them on into the green world still.

Susan Underwood

God as the Nest of Rabbits We Girls Found While Camping at My Cousin Carmen's

How many ways had the living world
played for our attention?
Fluorescent-green inchworms light as eyelashes
dropped from twigs right onto our forearms.
Swallowtail butterflies lit their yellow on our fingertips.
They pulsed open and closed in their way of saying our names.
Around our bodies on the yard, onto our bodies,
tasseling pink mimosa blossoms fell and fell.
We believed
we had not learned how to pray.

Baby rabbits woke us somehow into hazy sunrise,
and drew us from our tent into the brambling field.
Evergreens stepped forward in the inching light,
not yet green. And just then we could see their green.
No one dared to claim a tiny rabbit for her own.
There was one for each of us, but look, we looked,
and left them whole together as they were meant.
Yet we could not keep from touching
and wanting to touch.
We all saw and felt and believed
what each one of us saw and felt and believed:
rabbits, warm in the chill, and unafraid of us, and real.
Even on a summer morning, our breathing went
the misted way breathing does
in a heaven of fog as daylight touches first gray.
We couldn't have known what to say.
The soft fog and the soft fur
changed places with us.

Mai Der Vang

After All Have Gone

I once carried my mollusk tune
All the way to the lottery of gods.

Rain was the old funeral choir
That keened of a hemisphere

Moored under lapwings.
Clouds never left. I knew

The lights would shine clearer
If I closed my eyes, just as

I knew the Pacific would teach
Me to sleep before tying my

Name to the flaming. Here I
Am now at the end of amethyst,

Drizzling another lost sunrise
Inside the quilt of your hand.

Irene Vázquez

Hothouse or, The Taking Back of the Provision Grounds

I DON'T MEAN TO
ALARM YOU BUT

WE ARE NOT ALONE IN OUR BODIES / I DON'T
MEAN TO ERASE YOUR AGENCY BUT / WE ARE
LESS BODIES THAN BOTANICAL GARDENS / LESS
INDIVIDUALS THAN A COLLECTION OF HOLY
SACRAMENTS / WHAT I MEAN IS / I RECENTLY
FOUND OUT THERE ARE TRILLIONS OF
MICROORGANISMS IN THE GUT ALONE /
BACTERIA VIRUSES & FUNGI / MORE THAN THE
NUMBER OF HUMAN CELLS IN THE

ENTIRE BODY

I

MEAN

I ALWAYS HAD A SNEAKING SUSPICION WE EXCEEDED THIS
ANATOMY / SUSTAINED BY SOMETHING SIMPLER AND PERHAPS,
CLOSER TO GOD / SOMETHING MORE ANCIENT THAT KNOWS
NO NAME / SOMETHING PASSED DOWN MORE PRECIOUS THAN
PROPERTY /

SO FUCK OFF BIG PHARMA

THESE IS OURS

WE GREW THEM OURSELVES OR
RATHER / MADE OF THE BODY A
HOTHOUSE / GAVE THEM A PLACE TO
GO WHERE THEY LIVE
COLLECTIVELY AND RENT FREE

WHEN I AM LONELY IN THIS
PANDEMIC EXISTENCE WE
HAVE BEGUN TO CALL A LIFE
/ I IMAGINE THEM ALL MISS
FRIZZLED UP IN MY DIGESTIVE
SYSTEM / ON A MAGIC SCHOOL
BUS RIDE IN THE TWIST &
TURNS OF MY INTESTINE /
I HOPE THEY LAUGH UP IN
THERE AND IT MAKES ME
GASSY / I HOPE THEY SNORT
LIKE MY BEST FRIEND MADDIE
/ I HOPE THEY RING OUT WHEN
THEY'VE WON AN ARGUMENT
LIKE SID / I HOPE THEY THROW
GROOVY PARTIES UP IN MY
GUT LIKE CAROLINE / IN
OTHER WORDS / I HOPE THEY
LIKE TO BOOGIE / ENGAGING
IN WHATEVA KIND OF
UNICELLULAR MOTION
FLOATS

THEY LITTLE
BACTERIAL BOAT!

AS I WRITE THIS POEM / I IMAGINE
THEM NOURISHED BY MY LATE
AFTERNOON SNACK / OR, WHATEVER
LEFTOVERS I EAT STANDING / IN MY
KITCHEN

AND AS LONG AS I AM HERE /
ANTHROPOMORPHIZING BACTERIA
THAT ARE NOT AWARE I HAVE A
CONSCIOUSNESS / LET ME JUST SAY /
OUR MICROBIOME HAS DONE MORE
FOR US THAN ANY PRESIDENT EVER
HAS, WHICH IS TO SAY / KEPT US
ALIVE ON PURPOSE /

DARE I SAY THAT OUR BACTERIA
KNOW THAT RACE IS A FICTION BUT
THEY TOO HAVE SEEN SOME SHIT GO
DOWN ON THE PROVISION GROUNDS
/ THEY HAVE KNOWN POISONED
WATERS THAT PRECEDED US / &
THEY WILL BE BETTER PREPARED
FOR WHATEVER FUTURE THAT IS TO
COME /

WHEN I AM AT MY LOWEST / I HEAR THEM CALLING TO US / O, OUR CHILDREN
OF LOUISIANA SILT / DELTA BABIES, UNBOUGHT / AND UNBOSSED / WE WISH
YOU MUD AND MUCK / FROM YOUR MOTHERS WE WERE FORMED / NOT BORN
BUT GUIDING YOU THROUGH YOUR JOURNEY BACK TO THE EARTH / TO THE MUD
ONE DAY / WE WILL RETURN / BOTH BEYOND & BECAUSE OF YOU / BUT HERE,
IN THE POEM WE CAN BE ANYTHING / SO WE SYNTHESIZED VITAMINS AND GAVE
YOU RHYTHM / BROKE DOWN SIMPLE CARBOHYDRATES & SENT YOU MOXIE / WE
PUSHED & PULLED YOU TO THE BEAT OF OUR ANCESTORS TO GIVE YOU THIS / THE
GOD BODY

SO WHEN WE EAT NOW / WE EAT SACRAMENT /
WHEN WE LIVE NOW / WE LIVE GARDEN / WHEN
WE FUCK / & JUMP / & SLEEP SOUNDLY IN THE
NIGHT / WE ARE BOUNTIFUL / WE ARE MULTIPLE
/ WE ARE HOME

Joe Wilkins

Explain: Wolves

*OR-7, also known as Journey, is the first confirmed wolf in
western Oregon since 1947, and the first in California since 1924.
Since the wolf left his pack in September 2011, he has wandered
more than 1,000 miles . . . through Oregon and Northern
California.*

— WIKIPEDIA

The wandering wolf OR-7 appears to have a mate.

— OREGONIAN, MAY 12, 2014

She wanders heavy-bellied, full of milk & knives.
Lowers the barrel of her body like this, forepaws soft & sure as
      motherwings against the infant earth.
When finally she takes flight, she falls to gnashing the neckmeat of deer,
      one last upwelling of arterial blood the very blush of certain
      bodies in the near heavens.
When mountains gather their snap & shatter, when down comes the
      wind & winterlong, even wolfbones leak their autumn grease,
      wolfeyes go lonesome & sallow, & for warmth every wolf snouts
      the yeasting fleshpockets of those they run with & love.
I'm telling you capped & nightgowned like that the story is not the wolf's
      but ours, our fear not of being devoured but blinded, lied to, made
      complicit in our own undoing.
I'm telling you if he came through the bedsheets & afternoon light after
      you, then, yes, I'd do whatever wild, spine-breaking thing was in
      me to do.
I'm telling you if we ever on the next ridge see her loping down the scree,
      teats swinging, or in the fireblind night hear above the sough &
      slap of lakewater his dark bell of howl boom & ring, then children
      we will lean into one another, into our own itching hides, all the
      lengths of our glad, animal bones.

Corrie Williamson

Mercy Me

said the womenfolk where I was raised, and in my mind
mercy was a verb, the action reflexive. Though of course
      the wolf in the kingdom of winter does not mercy
the elk. The owl does not mercy the hare
that has trembled loose from its delicate coat of stillness.
      The word's been used since the twelfth century to mean
God's forgiveness of his creatures' offenses.
Such mercy is not what my father had in mind
      when he asked me to take a pistol to live
in the wilderness. I didn't. That was not
how I imagined my days, strapping its cold weight
      to my hip, a saunter to the river: *Good morning*
larkspur, good morning death camas and moon-
flower: I am more deadly than you. Would I
      slip it into the crook of the quince tree while
I crouched to weed kale? And would I, after all,
shoot a bear eclipsing my doorway? Would I
      shoot a man?   Back home, another gun
in the safe where my bedroom dresser used to stand.
Out there, the news, a loaded gun, returns again
      and again to the loaded gun. Here
the old growth murmurs at night, the dark's bones
groan and creep. Once, barefoot in starlight
      the color of gingerroot, trembling on the porch
at the unknowable's cacophony, the dog in a huff,
I wondered if the fear, in the end, would get me
      first. On the long, hawk-spangled
drive east, all things appeared to me as bodies: the log
haulers piled with the fallen forms of fir
      coming down from the mountains, chicken trucks
with their live cargoes crushed into hunchback
and the smashed daises of feathers from which
      a dim red eye looks out. Across the frostbit

flatlands of Idaho, gleaming silver trucks piled
with fleshy potatoes: bodies, bodies, and on the radio
          a story about a body unearthed from high
in the Andes, a woman's form arrayed with spear
and ax-head, a big-game hunter. I want to summon
          a blessing on this vanishing year—but I forget how
this works, what to say,   in what order.
I'm thinking of my good Aunt Sue who for all
          those years and even after the chemo and the electro-
shock therapy tucked her pale delicate chin at table
and said with quavering but without irony: *We give*
          thanks.   The moon's between the fir's ribs,
up there in the god-dark black. The fox still moves
in the roots and the rust.   You could say and not lie
          that this is most of what I long for in the way
of distance and the way of desire: may the fetters
fall from all of us this year. May the wild light
          get way down in our bones. May we, without
requital, mercy one another with hands like wings,
                    with unarmed hands.

Cathy Wittmeyer

Genesis 2:20

what is it you are up to / noisily plodding this paisley path— / plodding, plotting— / the conquering / a naming of all that / you don't own / as you unsettle deer / quietly foraging nettles, yarrow, clover / good morning, lovelies / you say / you name those whom / you do not at all own / and you graced your own / babes with given names / yet you call them / pumpkin / but you do not own them / either or the lovesick thrushes / playing hide-and-go-seek— / you don't say blackbird but / hi, babies / even though your own / womb played no mother / to this—magnificence— / your ugly boots plod / past a paddock and / you diminutize a herculean palomino with / hello, horsey / and grazing auburn heifers / adorable methane-gassers you call / cute / cute milk—or—steak / and last night's rain drips / off st. john's wort's golden face / don't cry, cupcake you coo / even rabbit or horse / or flower or fox / are too much to utter / try brother / try sister / (not mother) / better aunt or uncle / or how about— god— / for this is good / and your delight childlike / be like the tree / the moss you pet / stay silent / diminish not / that which cannot be named / —not again— / after that original taxonomy / you claim a power / use the miniature as if it owes you / its grackle its growl / its buzz its hum / maybe it calls you / baby / in your spring dress / moss dress / baby doll dress / within the bounds / of your bones / of your flesh / of your ignorance / and it starts to rain / smell past a carcass's remnants / a cat perhaps / a fox got her / feral cats that don't belong here / eating young wrens / poor babies / the cat's purr sounds just like / the wingbeats of a songbird / did you know that / heavy-booted plodder calling / here, kitty kitty / eden is a backyard / eden is a rooftop garden / eden is fenced in / eden is plowed under / eden is asphalted / eden is a warbler's nest / stop calling the nuthatch / honeybun / it doesn't call you / sweetie-pie / surely it has another name / you can / not understand / you adam / you eve / you little god

Karenne Wood

from The Naming

Some nights we feel the furred darkness
of an ancient one's breath and are trapped
in awakening, dismembered
by events we no longer recall.
We can touch the windowsill,
where October air gathers
as hours slip past in thin robes,
the forest a concert of voices.
The last crickets let go of their songs.

The land speaks, its language arising
from its own geography—
the mountains' hulked shapes
are blue whales, remembering
when they were undersea ridges,
and rivers are serpentine strands
hammered from silver, and dark trees
talk to the wind—weaving mortal lives,
drumbeats, pillars of smoke,
voices wavering into updraft,
the storyteller shifting the present.

Diana Woodcock

Hippocampus (Bent Horse)

If only you could enter our turf without riffling it;
if you had ears to hear the songs we sing
among corals and clouds. We are Lemon-

yellow *Hippocampus kudas*, against blue
Arabian Gulf waters and dying corals—
our poised movements through waters medicine

for a stressed soul, shaping meaning out of chaos
as we float and pirouette in obedience to the sea,
asserting our silent song by mere movement,

resolving all contradictions of consciousness,
our sublime presence a wordless rhyme—bent
horses with flared nostrils, long narrow muzzles

like purebred Arabian beauties.
Uprightly swimming, fluttering dorsal fins
propelling us elegantly through shallow waters.

See us in seagrass beds, our life stations,
tubular snouts sucking up small crustaceans.
Miniature, dainty dragons are we, smoke-breathing

as clouds of crushed food particles escape our gills.
Masters of camouflage, we change chameleonlike
from bright to mellow hues, grow long skin appendages

to blend in with algae, welcome encrusting beings
to settle on us. Monogamous couples gracefully
sailing through calm waters, we transform from brown

or green to a pale shade of cream. Watch our mating
ritual underwater: ballet twirling or entwining tails,
colors flashing, heads moving in unison. We males

with our brood pouches invite impregnation.
In captivity, we would die within a day
of our mate's passing. Vulnerable to trawling

and dredging, we are victims of aquarium keepers
and China's seekers after aphrodisiacs. Beyond
the surf of plastic bags and water bottles,

drift into an underworld of diamond-
studded sands, light and dispersed fireworks;
descend in reverse—kitelike—floating among

reflected clouds and seagrasses, searching
for us dainty dancers, elegant prancers.
Watch us come floating, picking up our pace

to catch a fleck of food, then gliding and
glowing in the spotlight of a sun that reaches
down from on high to bless us whom you,

if your heart is tender,
        will safeguard all
                this livelong day.

William Woolfitt

The Night the Rain Had Nowhere to Go

the third angel poured out his vial upon the rivers
— MARIA GUNNOE

Before wanted posters were hung   her name & face   at gas stations
& the Magic Mart   Before she testified   to the House Subcommittee
on Energy and Mineral Resources   made congressmen look

at her slides   orange creeks   scummy tap water   a nude girl bathing
in mine waste   Before capitol police   detained   interrogated her
for an hour   Before she told reporters   *I'm a hillbilly   a Cherokee*

a fierce mother   Before the ridge behind her house   was blasted
& her children   got nosebleeds from the dust   had to play inside
Before strangers gave her children the finger   taunted them   Before

coal trucks swerved   tried to run her off the road   Before the sand
in her gas tank   & knifed tires   There was the night the rain came
moaning down   had nowhere to go   valley fills near her house

had been packed with debris   everywhere the soil was pressed down
a great grinding flood   Big Branch Creek   took her access bridge
her walkway   She left her kids   in their house   tried to climb

the hill   tried for higher ground   couldn't push through   the slosh of
liquid mud   the hill washing down on her   her feet sunken
slipping in mud   the earth sliding away

Ellen June Wright

Who's to say my body is not all the world

after Francine J. Harris

is there a wetland inside me
        an ecosystem all its own
                so many species of chlorophyll-filled
                    flora and doelike fauna
            living symbiotically within
        some recess of my body

who is to say I am not Mother Earth
        home to lizard and the toad
            home to slick-black catfish
        that swim and *wriggle* upon the land

who's to say my big, brown
        body is not the whole world
            with its hemispheres, equator
                its longitude and latitude
        its mighty meridian

who is to say no wild dogs roam in me
        who is to say I am not part wolf
            or I am not the valleys upon
                which the hunched-back buffalo now graze
        as its numbers grow

Kenton K. Yee

The Big One

after Stanley Kunitz

Sister Maria in third grade homeroom
told us to disregard the rumor
that the San Andreas fault
will level The City's masonry
including our Chinatown schoolhouse
Thursday morning, after which
there will be no school,
no tests, no homeworks due
forever. Channel 7 interviewed
a Caltech seismologist with
wavy hair and glasses thick as
those I'm wearing now who
said, Don't trust psychic
predictions, but it's always advisable
to store water and provisions
and take cover under a door frame
when the Big One—which
I'm not predicting for Thursday morning—
comes. Feeling sad Wednesday night
that the oxtail stew could be the last
meal I'd share with Grandpa,
who sleeps in a brick masonry
walk-up, I washed it down with
my mother's melon soup and,
without even bidding Grandpa goodbye,
withdrew to my room where
I couldn't diagram the sentences
assigned, so sure was I
there would be no school
anymore. Thursday, weeks, years, and
Grandpa passed. I left to attend Caltech
and came back. Small ones. 9/11. Two

wars. Three Giants World Series.
Still, no Big One. Look for me, Grandpa,
in a seismic retrofitted building
stocked with water and provisions.
I'm the grim boy in a faded tee
and molasses glasses scribbling in bed,
glancing at the door frame
once a minute, listening
for the coming of your cane.

Monica Youn

A Guide to Usage: Mine

<u>A. Pronoun</u>

My.

Be-
longing

to me.

> *how should I define the limits of my concern the boundary between*
> *mine and not-mine the chime of the pronoun like a steel ring cast over*
> *what I know what I name what I claim what I own the whine of the*
> *pronoun hones its bright edges to keenness because there is power in the*
> *categorical that prides itself and plumps itself and proliferates till there*
> *is no room in here for anything but power till there is no air in here but*
> *there would be no need for air if you could learn to breathe in whatever*
> *I breathe out*

<u>B. Noun 1</u>

A pit or tunnel in

the earth
from which
precious

stones or ores or coal
are taken

by digging
or by other methods.

> *because the earth does not gleam with the shine of the noun to dig*
> *into the earth is imperative to use my fingers or else to fashion more*
> *rigid more perdurable fingers that cut or delve or sift or shatter because*
> *we are more evolved than animals because to mine is not to burrow*
> *because the earth is not for us to live in because the earth is not precious*
> *in itself the earth is that from which what is precious is taken the earth*
> *is what is scraped away or blasted away or melted away from what my*
> *steeltipped fingers can display or sell or burn*

C. Noun 2

A device
intended

to explode
when stepped upon
or touched,

or when approached by
a ship, vehicle,

or person.

> *my devise my device redefined by intent so thinskinned this earth is*
> *untouchable a sly simulacrum of innocence concealing an infinity of*
> *hairtrigger malice the cry of the noun sealed in a concentric sphere*
> *that sheathes its lethal secret in silence unapproachable it sings its*
> *unspeakable harvest in this field I have seeded with violence*

D. Verb

To dig
away or otherwise remove

the substratum
or foundation
of.

To sap.
To ruin

by slow degrees or secret means.

> *to dig is to build dark dwellings of negative space to knit a linked*
> *network of nothing the seams of the seemingly solid unravel the itch*
> *of erosion the scratch of collapse each absence the artifact of specific*
> *intention an abscess a crater a honeycomb of dead husks the home of*
> *the verb is founded on ruin the crime of the verb hollows out prisons*
> *and graves the rhyme of the verb tunnels from fissure to fracture from*
> *factory to faction from faultline to fate this foundation is equal parts*
> *atom and emptiness this fear invades fractally by rhizome and root*
> *what cement could salvage this crumbling concrete should I pledge my*
> *allegiance to unearthing or earth*

Felicia Zamora

Ecogodliness

The gutter drools a slow drip
& this baptism of storm crawls

back into lips of clouds, licks
tonsils of sky to esophagus

of atmosphere—you comb
wet grasses with fingers & palms.

Soon. Reduction to damp, reduction
to dry. What beloved we beyond

a summoning of desires: rain
to soak the drought, drought

to drain the flood, flood finch's song
to unravel the funnel cloud's hatch

across a prairie horizon. Psalm
exists here—in gaps between want

& fathom. You unknow the robin's
egg bundles in nest or smashes at tree's

rooted base. *Know.* Palmistry sews within
your pericardium. *Unknow:* a giving

of sinew & self over to the elements. Be
element as element. *Unlearn:* any

birthrights: all passages. Psalm exists
where wind awakens bark & branch

to beckon a wave of limbs, forest
full of chorus, *Here here, belong with us.*

Jessica Zhou

Southeastern Expansion

the flight from san francisco, to
miami is about 6 hours; in that
time, you can walk along the pe
rimeter of golden gate park 2.5
times, from lands' end to embarca
dero 2.5 times. what is the shape of
violence? i am not sure, but here i
am, still, some how, witnessing my
self from the distance. i love you
as an edifice, i think, just as mu
ch as i love the stories i tell my
self in the mirror. will you drink
thai iced tea with me when the
sky turns turns the same color?
can you stay when there are free
lunches, no longer? did you know
the people who made you your lun
ches? when you go out to walk your
newly-adopted pup, will you look
the one in need of a home, in the eye?
or are we too preoccupied with the amer
ican dream of home ownership? or the o
ther american dream, of striking it rich, of
this century's goldrush, as the city's luster, a
self, washes away? in other wor/l/ds, freeways
split the panhandle and golden gate park, wher
e the salesforce tower is dwarfed by others. what
is a consumer to a city? i am not sure, but it could
have something to do with the excess of a moveout.
an abandoning of something after it ceases to be a
ble to serve you. an off-season flight of immigrant pa
rrots, eating buds and blossoms. an earthquake, maxi
mum mercalli intensity of xi, levelling the ci
ty in 1906. whenever i meet someone wh
o grew up in california, it's like, we
speak in simile so naturally;
and we are, like, ourselves,
our lives, lived, in parallel,
to sunshine, rain fog, fire,
and earthquake.

Southeastern Expansion (*continued*)

Fiber cables that deliver the internet to Florida line the coast and are projected to be underwater by 2033. They are part of the estimated four thousand miles of fiber optic cable along other U.S. coastlines that will be underwater by 2030.

Karl Zuelke

Cat o' the Mountain

Low clouds hold snow
Over the shrouded stream, clear as a bite
Where trout hover smooth and still
In a fixed current
And aspen branches yellow
In the clutch of the hushed, cold season.
The eagle hangs on his black wings
Eye set on something small
A mile off.
            Where to begin?
Which river fork, which intricate split
Of the mountain grasses placed
Just so by hoofs of mule deer?
Which foot—waiting, frozen—
Waiting to freeze?
The cat o' the mountain yawns
Crosses the clearing.
Aspens tremble.

Jane Zwart

I read that the moon is rusting

My son defines time—its river, not its measure—
as the way one event changes into another.

I am letting what my son knows of time
climb and turn a laddered wheel in my mind.

I am letting the river run the mill that changes
one kind of unknowing into another.

+

Once a student told me that her mother kept
vases of flowers long past their prime.

She thought them still beautiful, wizened tulips,
their petals knuckling into pecans.

+

I read that the moon is rusting. Here on earth
a breeze kicked up by passing cars

fans a dead katydid. Invisible thumbs shuffle
her wings' gauzy underthings.

+

One event is turning into another. My son grows
tall but is still young enough to trail

a hand, offhandedly, in the current that carries him.
There is so little we can demand of time

but I would ask to be like a tulip, like a katydid,
like the henna-chinned moon:

one of those who, done or undone, changes next
into another kind of wonder.

CONTRIBUTORS' NOTES

ANN FISHER-WIRTH is the author of several poetry collections, including *Paradise Is Jagged, The Bones of Winter Birds, Mississippi,* and *Carta Marina.* A senior fellow of the Black Earth Institute, she is the 2023 recipient of the Governor's Award for Excellence in Poetry from the Mississippi Arts Commission. Her honors include the Malahat Review Long Poem Prize, the Rita Dove Poetry Award, three Mississippi Arts Commission Poetry fellowships, and the Mississippi Institute of Arts and Letters Poetry Prize. She is retired from the University of Mississippi, where she directed the minor in environmental studies.

LAURA-GRAY STREET is the author of *Pigment and Fume* and *Shift Work* and coeditor of *The Ecopoetry Anthology and A Literary Field Guide to Southern Appalachia.* Her poetry has received prizes from the *Greensboro Review,* the Dana Awards, *Isotope,* and *Terrain.org* and has been supported by fellowships from the Virginia Commission for the Arts, the Virginia Center for the Creative Arts, the Hambidge Center for the Arts and Sciences, and Storyknife. A fellow of the Black Earth Institute, Street is a professor of English at Randolph College, directs the school's Visiting Writers Series, and edits *Revolute,* the MFA program's literary journal.

CAMILLE DUNGY is the poetry editor for *Orion,* host of the podcast *Immaterial,* and University Distinguished Professor at Colorado State University. She is the author of *Soil: The Story of a Black Mother's Garden* and four collections of poetry.

MARGARET RONDA is the author of *Remainders: American Poetry at Nature's End* and the poetry collections *Personification* and *For Hunger.* She teaches at the University of California, Davis.

SANTIAGO ACOSTA is an assistant professor at Yale University and the recipient of the José Emilio Pacheco Literature Prize for his poetry collection *El próximo desierto* (The Coming Desert).

KELLI RUSSELL AGODON is the author of *Dialogues with Rising Tides*. She is a bi/queer poet and editor from the Pacific Northwest.

HUSSAIN AHMED is a Nigerian poet and environmentalist. He is the author of *Soliloquy with the Ghosts in Nile* and a doctoral student at the University of Cincinnati.

ASHIA AJANI is the author of *Heirloom: Collected Poems*.

ELLERY AKERS is the author of *A Door into the Wild: Poetry and Art* and *Swerve: Poems on Environmentalism, Feminism, and Resistance* and three other poetry collections.

RUTH AWAD is a Lebanese American poet, the author of *Outside the Joy* and *Set to Music a Wildfire,* and the recipient of a National Endowment for the Arts fellowship.

SUBHAGA CRYSTAL BACON is a queer elder from rural Washington and the author of *Transitory, Surrender of Water in Hidden Places,* and two other books.

DAVID BAKER is the author of *Whale Fall, Swift: New and Selected Poems,* and *Show Me Your Environment.* He has taught in America and Europe and lives in Granville, Ohio.

NED BALBO is the author of *The Cylburn Touch-Me-Nots* and *3 Nights of the Perseids* and has received grants from the National Endowment for the Arts and the Maryland Arts Council.

STACEY BALKUN is the author of *Sweetbitter* and coeditor of *Fiolet and Wing: An Anthology of Domestic Fabulist Poetry.* Her work has appeared in the *Mississippi Review* and *Pleiades.*

MILDRED KINONCO BARYA is a North Carolina–based writer and poet of East African descent. Her poetry collections include *The Animals of My Earth School.*

JANÉE J. BAUGHER is the author of *The Ekphrastic Writer: Creating Art-Influenced Poetry, Fiction, and Nonfiction* and the poetry collections *The Body's Physics* and *Coördinates of Yes.*

ANNA LENA PHILLIPS BELL is the author of *Ornament* and the chapbook *Smaller Songs* and winner of the Vassar Miller Prize. She is also the editor of *Ecotone.*

JARED BELOFF is the author of *Who Will Cradle Your Head* and a teacher who lives in Queens, New York.

ARIANA BENSON is a southern Black ecopoet whose collection *Black Pastoral* received the Cave Canem Poetry Prize and was a finalist for the National Books Critics Circle Leonard Prize.

SHERWIN BITSUI is Diné of the Todich'ii'nii, the author of three poetry collections, and the recipient of a Whiting Award, an American Book Award, and a PEN Book Award.

ALLEN BRADEN's work has appeared in *Cascadia: A Field Guide through Art, Ecology, and Poetry* and *Dear Human at the Edge of Time: Poems on Climate Change in the United States.*

TINA MOZELLE BRAZIEL is the author of *Known by Salt*, which received the Philip Levine Prize, and the coauthor of *Glass Cabin*.

NICKOLE BROWN is the author of *Sister* and *Fanny Says*. She teaches in the Sewanee School of Letters MFA program and lives in Asheville, North Carolina.

B. J. BUCKLEY is a Montana poet who has worked in arts in the schools and community programs for five decades. Her most recent books are *Flyover Country* and *Night Music*.

SIMMONS BUNTIN is the author of the poetry collections *Bloom* and *Riverfall* and the essay collection *Satellite: Essays on Fatherhood and Home, Near and Far.* He is the founding editor of *Terrain.org*.

LAUREN CAMP serves as the poet laureate of New Mexico and is the author of eight books. She was astronomer-in-residence at Grand Canyon National Park.

WENDY TAYLOR CARLISLE lives and writes in the Arkansas Ozarks. She is the author of four books and five chapbooks.

ANDERS CARLSON-WEE is the author of *Disease of Kings* and *The Low Passions*, a New York Public Library book group selection.

EMOGENE CATALDO was raised in Minnesota and lives in New York City.

VICTORIA CHANG's most recent poetry collection is *With My Back to the World*. She has received a Guggenheim fellowship and the Chowdhury Prize in Literature.

ROBIN CHAPMAN's most recent poetry collection is *Panic Season.*

TERESA MEI CHUC is the author of the poetry collections *Invisible Light, Keeper of the Winds,* and *Red Thread*. She teaches English in Los Angeles.

ANTHONY CODY is the author of *Borderland Apocrypha*, a finalist for the National Book Award for poetry, and *The Rendering*. He has received a Whiting Award and an American Book Award.

DANIEL CORRIE is the author of the poetry collections *Words, World, For the Future,* and *Human.* He lives in Georgia.

BRITNEY CORRIGAN is the author of the poetry collections *Solastalgia, Daughters, Breaking, Navigation,* and *40 Weeks.* She lives in Portland, Oregon.

JASON B. CRAWFORD is the author of two poetry collections, most recently *YEET!,* which received the 2023 Omnidawn 1st/2nd Book Prize.

LAURA DA' is a poet and teacher. Her most recent book, *Instruments of the True Measure,* received the Washington State Book Award.

AIDAN DANIEL is a writer, teacher, and visual artist from Virginia.

NOAH DAVIS is the author of the poetry collections *The Last Beast We Revel In* and *Of This River.*

TODD DAVIS's most recent poetry collections are *Ditch Memory: New and Selected Poems* and *Coffin Honey.* He teaches at Penn State Altoona.

LUCILLE LANG DAY is the author or editor of twenty books, including *Birds of San Pancho and Other Poems of Place* and *Fire and Rain: Ecopoetry of California.*

JANINE DEBAISE is the author of *Bi Language* and *Of a Feather.* Her essays have appeared in *Orion, Southwest Review,* and *Prairie Schooner.*

NATALIE DIAZ is the author of the Pulitzer Prize–winning collection *Postcolonial Love Poem.* She is Mojave and an enrolled member of the Gila River Indian Tribe.

LATASHA N. NEVADA DIGGS is the author of *Village* and *TWERK.* She lives in El Barrio, on Lenape Territory near the Weckquaesgeek.

MICHAEL DOWDY is a poet and scholar whose books include *Urbilly, Broken Souths,* and *Tell Me about Your Bad Guys.* He teaches at Villanova University.

KENDALL DUNKELBERG's fourth poetry collection is *Tree Fall with Birdsong.* He edits *Poetry South* and directs the low-residency MFA program at Mississippi University for Women.

IRIS JAMAHL DUNKLE is the author of *West: Fire: Archive, Riding Like the Wind: The Life of Sanora Babb,* and *Charmian Kittredge London: Trailblazer, Author, Adventurer.*

THOMAS DUNN is a Cave Canem fellow, multimedia artist, and poet from Michigan.

TERESA DZIEGLEWICZ is the author of *Something Small of How to See a River,* a Black Earth Institute fellow, and poet-in-residence at the Chicago Poetry Center.

MARTÍN ESPADA's honors include the National Book Award for poetry for *Floaters*, a Ruth Lilly Prize, and a Guggenheim fellowship. He teaches at the University of Massachusetts.

MICHELLE BONCZEK EVORY is the author of *The Ghosts of Lost Animals*, winner of the Barry Spacks Poetry Prize, and an artist-in-residence at Gettysburg National Military Park. She teaches in Kalamazoo, Michigan.

ALYSON (AL) FAVILLA's work has appeared in *Poetry Ireland Review, Diode, Electric Literature, About Place,* and elsewhere.

BETH ANN FENNELLY's most recent book is *Heating and Cooling: 52 Micro-Memoirs*. She served as poet laureate of Mississippi from 2016 to 2021.

MOLLY FISK is the editor of *California Fire and Water: A Climate Crisis Anthology* and the recipient of an Academy of American Poets fellowship. She lives in the Sierra foothills.

VIEVEE FRANCIS is the author of *The Shared World, Forest Primeval,* and *Horse in the Dark*. She is an associate professor of English and creative writing at Dartmouth College.

CMARIE FUHRMAN is a writer and poet who lives in the Idaho mountains.

BENJAMIN GARCIA's collection *Thrown in the Throat* received the Eugene Paul Nassar Poetry Prize and was a finalist for the Kate Tufts Discovery Award.

MICHAEL GARRIGAN is the author of the poetry collections *River, Amen,* and *Robbing the Pillars*.

ROSS GAY is the author of numerous poetry and essay collections. *Catalog of Unabashed Gratitude* received the National Book Critics Circle Award and the Kingsley Tufts Poetry Award.

MELISSA GINSBURG is the author of four books, most recently *Doll Apollo*. Her work has appeared in the *New Yorker, Image,* and elsewhere. She teaches at the University of Mississippi.

SARAH GIRAGOSIAN is the author of the collections *The Death Spiral* and *Queer Fish,* which received the American Poetry Journal Book Prize. She teaches at the University at Albany.

JODY GLADDING is a translator and the author of five poetry collections, most recently *I entered without words*. She lives in East Calais, Vermont.

RIGOBERTO GONZÁLEZ is the author of seventeen books and the recipient of Lannan, Guggenheim, and National Endowment for the Arts fellowships and numerous literary honors.

ANDREW GOTTLIEB is the author of the poetry collection *Tales of a Distance* and has been a writer-in-residence in Denali, Everglades, and Isle Royale National Parks.

ROBIN GOW is a trans poet from rural Pennsylvania and the author of several poetry collections, including *Lanternfly August*, an essay collection, and a young adult novel in verse.

MAGGIE GRABER is the author of *Swan Hammer*, which received the Wheelbarrow Poetry Prize. She lives and teaches in Oxford, Mississippi.

DANA J. GRAEF has published articles and essays on wildness, mining, and climate change. Her creative work has appeared in *Rust & Moth* and *Split Rock Review*.

MIRIAM BIRD GREENBERG is the author of *In the Volcano's Mouth* and the recipient of a National Endowment for the Arts fellowship. She teaches at the University of California, Berkeley.

LILACE MELLIN GUIGNARD is the author of the memoir *When Everything beyond the Walls Is Wild: Being a Woman Outdoors in America*. Her poems have appeared in *Poetry* and elsewhere.

KELSEA HABECKER is the author of the poetry collections *Hollow Out, The Walrus Wives*, and *North Wife* and the coauthor of *How to Write Poetry: A Guided Journal with Prompts*.

AARON HAND is the host of the *Personhood Project* poetry podcast. His work has appeared in *Poem-a-Day*, the *San Antonio Express-News*, and the *Houston Chronicle*.

EMAN HASSAN's poetry collection *Raghead* was an editor's pick in the New Issues Poetry & Prose First Book Award and a finalist for an Oregon Literary Award.

GISELA HEFFES is a writer and a professor of Latin American literature and culture at Johns Hopkins University. Her most recent creative book is *Aquí no hubo ni una estrella*.

KATHLEEN HELLEN is the author of two chapbooks and the poetry collections *Meet Me at the Bottom, The Only Country Was the Color of My Skin*, and *Umberto's Night*.

W. J. HERBERT's work appears in *Dear Specimen, The Atlantic, Best American Poetry, Georgia Review, Hudson Review*, and *Southern Review*.

CLAUDIA D. HERNÁNDEZ was born and raised in Guatemala. Her memoir *Knitting the Fog* received the Louise Meriwether First Book Prize.

TIFFANY MARGARET HIGGINS is a Fulbright scholar and a Pulitzer Rainforest Journalism Fund recipient.

SEAN HILL is the author of the poetry collections *Dangerous Goods* and *Blood Ties and Brown Liquor*. He is a professor of creative writing at the University of Montana.

RICK HILLES is the author of *Brother Salvage, A Map of the Lost World,* and *My Roberto Clemente*. He is an associate professor at Vanderbilt University.

CAROLINE HOCKENBURY is a poet and nonfiction writer from Kentucky.

CYNTHIA MARIE HOFFMAN is the author of the poetry collections *Exploding Head, Call Me When You Want to Talk about the Tombstones, Paper Doll Fetus,* and *Sightseer*.

MARYBETH HOLLEMAN is the author of *tender gravity, The Heart of the Sound,* and *Among Wolves*. She lives in the Chugach Mountains of Alaska.

ERIN COUGHLIN HOLLOWELL is a poet in Alaska. Her collections include *Pause, Traveler, Every Atom,* and *Corvus and Crater*.

MARIE HOWE is the author of four poetry collections. She is a chancellor of the Academy of American Poets and served as poet laureate of New York from 2012 to 2014.

RICHARD JACKSON is the author of more than thirty books and the recipient of Guggenheim, National Endowment for the Arts, and National Endowment for the Humanities fellowships.

JESSICA JACOBS is the founder and executive director of the literary nonprofit Yetzirah. Her third book, *unalone*, is a collection of poems in conversation with Genesis.

ELIZABETH JACOBSON is the author of *There Are as Many Songs in the World as Branches of Coal* and an Academy of American Poets Laureate fellow.

JACQUELINE JOHNSON is a multidisciplinary artist creating in poetry and fiber arts and the author of *A Woman's Season, On Main Street Rag Press,* and *A Gathering of Mother Tongues*.

TAYLOR JOHNSON is the author of *Inheritance* and the poet laureate of Takoma Park, Maryland. A Cave Canem fellow and the recipient of a Whiting Award, he lives in Washington, DC.

EVER JONES is the author of *Transanything, nightsong,* and *Wilderness Lessons* and teaches at the University of Washington, Tacoma.

KASEY JUEDS is the author of the poetry collections *The Thicket* and *Keeper,* which received the Agnes Lynch Starrett Prize.

JOAN NAVIYUK KANE's collection *Dark Traffic* was a finalist for the Kingsley Tufts poetry award. A Guggenheim fellow and Whiting Award recipient, Kane is Inupiaq.

JULIA SPICHER KASDORF is the author of five poetry collections, most recently *As Is*. With Steven Rubin, she created *Shale Play: Poems and Photographs from the Fracking Fields*.

ATHENA KILDEGAARD is the author of six books of poetry, including *Prairie Midden*, which received the WILLA Literary Award. She teaches at the University of Minnesota, Morris.

GRANT KITTRELL is the author of the poetry collection *Let's Sit Down, Figure This Out* and recipient of the Philip Booth Poetry Prize. He teaches at Randolph College.

SOPHIE KLAHR is the author of *Two Open Doors in a Field* and *Meet Me Here at Dawn* and the coauthor of *There Is Only One Ghost in the World*.

CHRISTOPHER KONDRICH is the author of *Valuing* and the coeditor of *Creature Needs: Writers Respond to the Science of Animal Conservation*.

BRANDON KRIEG is the author of *Magnifier*, which received the Colorado Prize for Poetry. He teaches at Kutztown University.

PETRA KUPPERS is a disability culture activist, poet, filmmaker, community performance artist, and recipient of a Guggenheim fellowship. She teaches at the University of Michigan.

JOE M. LAMB's poetry and essays have appeared in *Earth Island Journal*, *The Sun*, *Caliban*, *Wind*, and *Orion*. He is the founder of the Borneo Project.

JOHN LANE's collection *Abandoned Quarry: New and Selected Poems* received the Southeastern Independent Booksellers Alliance poetry book of the year.

J. DREW LANHAM is an academic, poet, and author. His honors include the Southern Book Prize, a MacArthur fellowship, and the Southern Environmental Law Center Reed Award.

DEBORAH LEIPZIGER is the Brazilian-born author of *Story and Bone*.

JULIA LEVINE's most recent book is *Ordinary Psalms*. She is an Academy of American Poetry Poet Laureate fellow.

ROSSY LIMA is the author of three poetry collections and two children's books and the recipient of the Americas Poetry Festival of New York's Poet of the Year Award.

ADA LIMÓN is the author of six books of poetry, including *The Carrying*, winner of the National Book Critics Circle Award. She serves as the twenty-fourth U.S. poet laureate.

LAYLI LONG SOLDIER is an Oglala Lakota poet, artist, and activist. Her poetry collection *Whereas* received the PEN/Jean Stein Book Award.

SANDY LONGHORN is the author of three poetry collections, most recently *The Alchemy of My Mortal Form*, and teaches in the Arkansas Writer's MFA Workshop at the University of Central Arkansas.

ÉIREANN LORSUNG is the author of *Music for Landing Planes By, Her book*, and *The Century*.

LEA MARSHALL's work has appeared in *Linebreak, Unsplendid, Hayden's Ferry Review, B O D Y, Diode, Thrush Poetry Journal*, and *Broad Street Magazine*. She lives in Virginia.

JENNIFER MARTELLI is the author of *The Queen of Queens* and *My Tarantella*, a Massachusetts Cultural Council fellow, and poetry coeditor for *MER*.

AIREA D. MATTHEWS is the author of *Simulacra* and teaches at Bryn Mawr College. She has served as Philadelphia's poet laureate and is the recipient of Pew and Guggenheim fellowships.

JANET MCADAMS is the author of *Feral* and *The Island of Lost Luggage*, which received the American Book Award, and the chapbook *Seven Boxes for the Country After*.

ANNE HAVEN MCDONNELL teaches at the Institute of American Indian Arts. She is the author of *Breath on a Coal* and the chapbook *Living with Wolves*.

ROSE MCLARNEY is the author of four poetry collections, most recently *Colorfast*. She is a professor at Auburn University and the editor of *Southern Humanities Review*.

LUCIEN DARJEUN MEADOWS is the author of *In the Hands of the River*. He has received awards from the Academy of American Poets and American Association of Geographers.

RAJIV MOHABIR is a poet, translator, and memoirist in Boulder, Colorado.

DANIELA NAOMI MOLNAR is an artist, poet, pigment worker, wilderness guide, and educator.

SAWNIE MORRIS is the author of *Her, Infinite* and *Matapolvo Rain*, cofounder of Amigos Bravos: Because Water Matters, and the inaugural poet laureate of Taos, New Mexico.

AIMEE NEZHUKUMATATHIL is the author of six books. Her honors include National Endowment for the Arts and Guggenheim fellowships. She teaches at the University of Mississippi.

JANUARY GILL O'NEIL is the author of *Glitter Road, Rewilding, Misery Islands,* and *Underlife.* She is an associate professor at Salem State University.

CECILY PARKS is the author of the poetry collections *The Seeds, O'Nights,* and *Field Folly Snow.* She teaches in the MFA program at Texas State University.

LYNN PATTISON's most recent poetry collection is *Matryoshka Houses.* Her work has appeared in the *Notre Dame Review, Pedestal, Moon City Review, Smartish Pace,* and *Ruminate.*

ANDREW PAYTON's poetry has appeared in *New Ohio Review, Nimrod, phoebe,* and *Masculinity: An Anthology of Modern Voices.* He lives in the Shenandoah Valley of Virginia.

TOMMY PICO is a poet, artist, and TV writer from the Viejas Indian reservation of the Kumeyaay Nation. His collection *Nature Poem* received an American Book Award.

CATHERINE PIERCE is the author of the poetry collections *Danger Days, The Tornado Is the World, The Girls of Peculiar,* and *Famous Last Words* and served as Mississippi's poet laureate.

ARLENE PLEVIN's poetry has appeared in Seattle's Poetry on the Buses program, *New Mexico Review, Global South,* and *Cabin Fever.*

VIVIAN FAITH PRESCOTT is a climate witness living in southeast Alaska in Lingít Aaní on the land of the Shtax'héen Kwáan. She writes poetry, nonfiction, and fiction.

JESSICA PURDY is the author of the chapbooks *The Adorable Knife* and *You're Never the Same: Ekphrastic Poems.*

JANE SATTERFIELD is the author of several poetry collections, including *The Badass Brontës* and *Apocalypse Mix,* and the recipient of a National Endowment for the Arts fellowship.

REBECCA SEIFERLE is a translator and the author of four poetry collections. She has served as poet laureate of Tucson and is the recipient of a Lannan literary fellowship.

ALAFIA NICOLE SESSIONS is the recipient of the Furious Flower Prize and the Sustainable Arts Foundation Award. She lives in Atlanta.

LEONA SEVICK's most recent poetry collection is *The Bamboo Wife.* She is provost and professor of English at Bridgewater College in Virginia.

SAMYAK SHERTOK's poems have appeared in *Poetry*, *Gettysburg Review*, and *Iowa Review*. His honors include the Robert and Adele Schiff Award and the Auburn Witness Prize.

JOHN SHOPTAW's most recent book is *Near-Earth Object*. He teaches poetry at the University of California, Berkeley.

MARTHA SILANO's most recent book is *Gravity Assist*. Her poems have appeared in *Poetry*, *American Poetry Review*, and the *Paris Review*.

DORSÍA SMITH SILVA is the author of *In Inheritance of Drowning*, the editor of *Latina/Chicana Mothering*, the poetry editor of *The Hopper*, and a professor at the University of Puerto Rico.

JAKE SKEETS is the author of *Eyes Bottle Dark with a Mouthful of Flowers*, which received the American Book Award. He is from the Navajo Nation and teaches at the University of Oklahoma.

DANEZ SMITH is the author of five poetry collections and has received fellowships from the McKnight Foundation, Cave Canem, and the National Endowment for the Arts.

TRACY K. SMITH is the author of five poetry collections, including *Life on Mars*, which received a Pulitzer Prize. A former U.S. poet laureate, she teaches at Harvard University.

HEIDI STAPLES is the author of five books, recipient of a New Issues Poetry Prize, and coeditor of *Big Energy Poets: When Ecopoetry Thinks Climate Change* and *Poets for Living Waters*.

PAGE HILL STARZINGER's book *Vortex Street* was shortlisted for the Eric Hoffer Grand Prize in Poetry. Her collection *Vestigial* received a Barrow Street Book Prize.

ROSE STRODE is a poet, essayist, and naturalist.

MARCELA SULAK is director of the graduate creative writing program at Bar Ilan University. Her work has been recognized by the Jewish Book Council and PEN.

HEATHER SWAN is the author of the poetry collections *A Kinship with Ash* and *Dandelion* and the nonfiction book *Where the Grass Still Sings: Stories of Insects and Interconnection*.

TESS TAYLOR is the author of five poetry collections. She lives near Berkeley, California.

BRIAN TEARE is the author of numerous books, including *Doomstead Days*. He lives in Charlottesville, Virginia, where he makes chapbooks by hand for his micropress, Albion Books.

ORCHID TIERNEY is the author of *A Year of Misreading the Wildcats* and *Looking at the Tiny*. Originally from New Zealand, she teaches at Kenyon College.

ALISON TOWNSEND is the author of *The Green Hour: A Natural History of Home, Persephone in America,* and *The Blue Dress*. Her work has appeared in *Best American Essays*.

NATASHA TRETHEWEY is the author of five collections of poetry, including *Native Guard*, which received the Pulitzer Prize. She served two terms as U.S. poet laureate.

BRIAN TURNER is the author of five collections of poetry, most recently *The Wild Delight of Wild Things*. He has received fellowships from the Guggenheim and Lannan Foundations.

SUSAN UNDERWOOD is the author of four poetry collections, most recently *Splinter*. Her novel *Genesis Road* received a Tennessee Arts Commission grant.

MAI DER VANG is the author of two poetry collections, most recently *Yellow Rain*, which received the Lenore Marshall Poetry Prize and an American Book Award.

IRENE VÁZQUEZ is a queer Black Mexican American poet, journalist, translator, and editor. Her chapbook is *Take Me to the Water*.

JOE WILKINS is the author of two novels, a memoir, and four poetry collections, including *Thieve* and *When We Were Birds*. He lives in western Oregon.

CORRIE WILLIAMSON is the author of the poetry collections *Your Mother's a Bear Gun, The River Where You Forgot My Name,* and *Sweet Husk*. She lives in Montana.

CATHY WITTMEYER hosts the Word to Action retreat in the Alps. She is the editor of the anthology *Eden Is a Backyard*.

KARENNE WOOD was a member of the Monacan Indian Nation and the author of the poetry collections *Markings on Earth* and *Weaving the Boundary*.

DIANA WOODCOCK is the author of *Heaven Underfoot* and teaches at Virginia Commonwealth University School of the Arts Qatar.

WILLIAM WOOLFITT is the author of four poetry collections, two story collections, and an essay collection. He is the founder and editor of *Speaking of Marvels*.

ELLEN JUNE WRIGHT is an American poet with British and Caribbean roots. Her work has appeared in *Plume, Tar River, Missouri Review, Verse Daily,* and *North American Review*.

KENTON K. YEE is a poet, fiction writer, physicist, and former professor at Columbia University. He lives in Northern California.

MONICA YOUN is the author of four poetry collections, most recently *From From*, which received the Anisfield Wolf Award.

FELICIA ZAMORA is an associate professor at the University of Cincinnati and the author of six poetry collections, including *I Always Carry My Bones*, which received the Iowa Poetry Prize.

JESSICA ZHOU lives in San Francisco.

KARL ZUELKE is the author of the poetry collection *Petting the Bumblebees*. He teaches at the Art Academy of Cincinnati.

JANE ZWART teaches at Calvin University, where she also codirects the Calvin Center for Faith and Writing. Her poems have appeared in *Poetry, TriQuarterly,* and *Ploughshares*.

ACKNOWLEDGMENTS AND CREDITS

I'd like to acknowledge the joy of collaborating once again with my coeditor and beloved friend Laura-Gray Street. I thank all the poets who shared their wonderful work with us, and all those who work at Trinity University Press for saying yes to this project. I also thank my husband, Peter Wirth, for his unending support and help, his knowledge of the other-than-human world, and the thousands of hours we have spent together in the woods. And I thank my children who are all, in their own ways, working to promote peace and environmental awareness in our world. And finally, thanks to Melissa Ginsburg for the phrase from her poem in this volume that we modified for the title *Attached to the Living World*.

— *Ann Fisher-Wirth*

I want to thank Ann Fisher-Wirth for the rich journey of coediting this anthology and its predecessor and our many collaborations through the years. Thank you for your friendship and for encouraging me in so many ways. Likewise, my husband, Jay Kardan, whose sharp eye and supportive love are my foundation. Thank you to my parents and my children, who ground me, past, present, and future. I am grateful to Randolph College, particularly for the sabbatical that allowed me to work on this anthology, and to my invaluable colleagues. And thank you to the water bodies, the beech trees, the white-tailed deer, the black bears, and all the birds that inhabit this snippet of the world with me. May the poems gathered here help that world in some possible way.

— *Laura-Gray Street*

sions Company, LLC, on behalf of Graywolf Press, Minneapolis, Minnesota, graywolfpress.org.

Heidi Staples, "Prayer" from *Noise Event* (Ahsahta Press, 2013). Reprinted with the permission of the author.

Page Starzinger, "Galaxy Filament" from *Vortex Street*. Copyright © 2020 by Page Starzinger. Reprinted with the permission of Barrow Street Press.

Marcela Sulak, "Lantana" from *Mouth Full of Seeds* (Black Lawrence Press). Copyright © 2020 by Marcela Sulak. Reprinted with the permission of the author.

Tess Taylor, "I. Rainy Season" and "IV. Escrow" from "California Suites" from *Rift Zone* (2020). Both reprinted with permission from Red Hen Press.

Brian Teare, "Toxics Release Inventory" from *Doomstead Days*. Copyright © 2019 by Brian Teare. Reprinted with the permission of Nightboat Books.

Brian Turner, "The Immortals" and "One Last Moment in the Vast City of Ants" from *The Wild Delight of Wild Things*. Copyright © 2023 by Brian Turner. Both reprinted with the permission of the Permissions Company, LLC, on behalf of Alice James Books, alicejamesbooks.org.

Mai Der Vang, "After All Have Gone" from *Afterland*. Copyright © 2017 by Mai Der Vang. Reprinted with the permission of the Permissions Company, LLC, on behalf of Graywolf Press, Minneapolis, Minnesota, www.graywolfpress.org.

Irene Vázquez, "Hothouse or, The Taking Back of the Provision Grounds" from *When Language Broke Open* (University of Arizona Press, 2023). Copyright © 2023 by Irene Vázquez. Reprinted with the permission of the author.

Joe Wilkins, "Explain: Wolves" from *Thieve* (Lynx House Press, 2019). Reprinted with the permission of the author.

Karenne Wood, "The Naming" from *Weaving the Boundary*. Copyright © 2016 by Karenne Wood. Reprinted by permission of the University of Arizona Press.

Diana Woodcock, "Hippocampus (Bent Horse)" from *Facing Aridity* (Homebound, 2021). Reprinted with the permission of the author.

Karl Zuelke, "Cat o' the Mountain" from *Petting the Bumblebee* (I-BeaM Books, 2019). Reprinted with the permission of the author.

The following poems are reprinted with the permission of the author: Santiago Acosta, "Never Surrender Your Heart to a Nuclear Power Plant"; Kelli Russell Agodon, "In the Next 50 Years So Many Animals Will Go Extinct It Will Take Earth at Least 3 Million Years to Recover"; Hussain Ahmed, "Talking Drums II"; Ashia Ajani, "Blue Cascade" and "Mint"; Ruth Awad, "Hunger" and "The Years of Water & Light"; Subhaga Crystal Bacon, "Warming, Cooling; Wet, Dry: Burning

Haibun"; Ned Balbo, "A Spell for Lamentation and Renewal" and "The Wolves of Chernobyl"; Mildred Kinonco Barya, "Cast Over Gorée Island"; Janée J. Baugher, "Andrew Wyeth's Footnotes to *Frosted Apples*, 1967" and "Andrew Wyeth's Footnotes to *The Carry*, 2003"; Anna Lena Phillips Bell, "Emerald"; Ariana Benson, "Black Pastoral" and "Love Poem in the Black Field"; Allen Braden, "Inspiration"; Tina Mozelle Braziel, "What the Creek Says"; Nickole Brown, "A Prayer to Talk to Animals" and "Collective Nouns for the Anthropocene"; B. J. Buckley, "Pronghorn Elegy"; Simmons Buntin, "Desert Cottontail"; Lauren Camp, "I've started naming the landscape: sweet" and "Echinopsis Pachanoi"; Wendy Taylor Carlisle, "May We in This Time"; Emogene Cataldo, "A question about procreation as the rivers dry"; Robin Chapman, "That slant of sun"; Teresa Mei Chuc, "Mother of Waters, River of Nine Dragons" and "Chernobyl Necklace"; Daniel Corrie, "Wiregrass, Bluestem, Indian Grass, Palmetto, Ferns, Wildflowers, Blackberry, Gallberry, Longleaf Pine, the Sweep of Fire"; jason b. crawford, "A Double Sonnet for the River"; Laura Da', "An Unknowable Creator Departs the Talking Fields" and "The Meadow Views: Sword and Symbolic History"; Aidan Daniel, "Virginia Possum Rages"; Noah Davis, "Poem Sewn into My Hunting Jacket"; Todd Davis, "Apostate"; Lucille Lang Day, "Lost Languages"; Michael Dowdy, "Blast Fragments"; Kendall Dunkelberg, "The intergalactic traveler in springtime" and "The intergalactic traveler tells it like it is"; Iris Jamahl Dunkle, "Black Blizzard" and "Disaster, a Reckoning"; Thomas Dunn, "It was raining"; Michelle Bonczek Evory, "By root, by petal, by sword"; Alyson Favilla, "Bullfrog"; Beth Ann Fennelly, "The Last Hummingbird of Summer"; Molly Fisk, "August"; Vievee Francis, "Clarity (for Those Who Do Nothing but Hope)" and "Cruelty"; CMarie Fuhrman, "End Times" and "Questioning the Sun"; Michael Garrigan, "Liturgy of Carp Becoming a God"; Ross Gay, "A Small Needful Fact"; Melissa Ginsburg, "So attached you are to living in the world"; Sarah Giragosian, "Newtok, Alaska"; Jody Gladding, "[grass widow / grass stained]"; Maggie Graber, "in which i notice the birds again"; Miriam Bird Greenberg, "• [Whole towns like • horses turnt loose]" and "• [In Paradise the fire ate]"; Lilace Mellin Guignard, "Fracked Pastoral"; Kelsea Habecker, "Self-Portrait with Salmon"; Aaron Hand, "Glimpses of Wilderness"; Eman Hassan, "To the Beach with My Nephew"; Gisela Heffes, "An Epistemology of Floriculture"; W. J. Herbert, "The End of Immortality"; Claudia D. Hernández, "The River Never Happened to Us (ii.)"; Tiffany Margaret Higgins, "Chewing the Sun"; Rick Hilles, "Tell Me"; Caroline Hockenbury, "Machete"; Cynthia Marie Hoffman, "Ecotherapy"; Marybeth Holleman, "she *zompopas*"; Erin Coughlin Hollowell, "Wrack Line" and "Choreographic"; Richard Jackson, "An Ending of Sorts"; Jacqueline Johnson, "Wild Life"; Taylor Johnson, from "Hymn"; Ever Jones, "Overheard from the Field"; Kasey Jueds, "The Vultures"; Athena Kildegaard, "Sudden"; Grant Kittrell, "the plan was to build the pipeline through my left lung"; Sophie Klahr, "Tender"; Christopher Kondrich, "Endling"; Joe M. Lamb, "Trinity"; John Lane, "Elegy for Sugar Sand and Slash Pine"; Deborah Leipziger, "Lobo"; Julia Levine, "Milk"; Sandy Longhorn, "The Crumple Zone"; Éireann Lorsung, "Garden cycle (keeping time)"; Lea Marshall, "Future Folk Tales: Fox" and "Future Folk Tales: Fireflies"; Jennifer Martelli, "Snakes"; Airea D. Matthews, "His Eye on the Sparrow"; Anne Haven McDonnell, "Inside a lateness, a singing under snow"; Lucien Darjeun Meadows, "Mile 57"; Sawnie Morris, "Frog Song"; Cecily Parks, "Girlhood"; Lynn Pattison, "When even the north grew too hot"; Andrew Payton, "War Road"; Arlene Plevin "Tikkun Olam"; Vivian Faith Prescott, "How to Yoik the Stikine River" and "At a nearby glacier, I heard a yoik for a child"; Jessica Purdy, "After Watching Lior Patel's 'Aerial Timelapse of Sheep Herding' and Søren Solkær's 'Amorphous Flocks of Starlings Swell above the Danish Marshlands'"; Rebecca Seiferle, "In the unending rain"; Alafia Nicole Sessions, "Love Poem as Omnipastoral"; Samyak Shertok, "The Last Beekeeper" and "A Brief History of Hunger"; John Shoptaw, "Pangolin Scales"; Martha Silano "Self-Portrait as Southern Resident Orca"; Dorsía Smith Silva, "Hurricane María Countdown" and "I pause to give gratitude to green"; Rose Strode, "Saint Cuthbert Proclaims the First Sanctuary for Birds, 676 A.D."; Heather Swan, "After"; Orchid Tierney, from "a field guide to future flora" [cottonwood or microfleece] and [flowers are slow-moving cows of the glebe]; Alison Townsend, "Northern Red Oak: Mercy"; Natasha Trethewey, "Elegy" [I think by now the river must be thick]; Susan Underwood, "God as the Nest of Rabbits We Girls Found While Camping at My Cousin Carmen's"; Corrie Williamson, "Mercy Me"; Cathy Wittmeyer, "Genesis 2:20"; William Woolfitt, "The Night the Rain Had Nowhere to Go"; Ellen June Wright, "who's to say my body is not all the world"; Kenton K. Yee, "The Big One"; Monica Youn, "A Guide to Usage: Mine"; Felicia Zamora, "Ecogodliness"; Jessica Zhou, "Southeastern Expansion"; Jane Zwart, "I read that the moon is rusting."